An

Animation

Mark Whitehead

www.pocketessentials.com

This edition published in June 2004 by Pocket Essentials,
P. O. Box 394, Harpenden, Herts, AL5 1JX
http://www.noexit.co.uk

A CIP catalogue record for this book is available from the British
Library.

ISBN 1 903047 46 3

2 4 6 8 10 9 7 5 3 1

Typography by Avocet Typeset, Chilton, Aylesbury, Bucks
Printed and bound in Great Britain by Cox & Wyman, Reading, Berks

Acknowledgements

Acme Instant Dehydrated Boulder Kits are due to Ion and Claire (for patience); Ian, Shannon, Vicky, Nick and Dave (for tolerance) and Karen, Claude, Miriam and Mum and Dad (for assistance).

Contents

Introduction:
The Child Receives a Lesson in a Twentyfourth of a Second

'Now take the art of animation. This may look a very simple movement, but do you realise it takes eight million separate drawings to make the lady's arm move from there . . . to there? It took one artist the best part of six years, working day and night, to complete that particular movement. And when he'd finished it the producer decided it wasn't needed in the finished film. The artist went away and shot himself.'

The Do It Yourself Cartoon Kit (1963)

It's a slight exaggeration but the effort that goes into producing animated movies never ceases to impress me. Even the worst examples, such as *The Care Bears Movie*, meant that some poor soul was slaving away over a light box, producing 24 frames a second of drawings for our edification. That takes a particular sort of dedication, a particular mind-set and particular willingness to suffer permanent eyestrain in order to keep people amused.

The director Frank Henenlotter was once interviewed about making *Basket Case*, a celebrated no-budget

gore movie from the early 1980s that featured a deform-
ed and evil twin who was kept in a basket by his more
normal-looking sibling. Originally, said Henenlotter,
they had planned to animate the creature with stop-
motion effects (moving it a little bit, filming it, moving it
a little bit more, filming it, and so on until it had cleared
the length of a room). They started off with the best of
intentions but, after a few hours of this with no great
reward, they resorted to throwing the creature across the
room and filming that instead. 'We thought about having
a credit for "ordinary effects" instead of special ones', he
said.

I can sympathise. In 1992, I attended a brief course on
animation at my local arts centre. We were each given a
Super 8 camera with single-frame advance and asked to
animate some household objects that we had found at the
centre. I came up with a box of rusty nails and a couple of
electrical plugs. My idea was to have the nails swarm out
of the box, engulf the plugs, dismantle them and free the
screws that held them together. It took me about eight
hours to get those fifteen seconds of action. Admittedly, I
kept breaking for cigarettes and tea. And swearing. Once
the footage was developed, I was quite impressed. It actually looked as I had wanted it to look. The nails swarmed,
the plugs were engulfed. You could see development.
Okay, so it was hardly Jan Švankmajer, but you could see
what was going on. It was at that moment that I realised
something very important. I had neither the inclination
nor the patience to ever be a successful animator, or even
an unsuccessful one, for that matter.

My ability to sit and watch animation remains undiminished however. Many of my earliest memories of TV are of animation. My fondness for Oliver Postgate's and Peter Firmin's output at Small Films remains undiminished. Postgate never talked down to his audience and his finest comment on producing children's television was the admirable: 'You've got to stretch the little buggers'. The eerie Švankmajeresque *Pogle's Wood*, the utopian small blue planet of *The Clangers*, the cod-Icelandic saga of *Noggin the Nog* and the folk traditions explored in *Bagpuss*, all of them are beautifully realised little worlds. It has become a cliché for thirtysomethings to get misty-eyed about the TV of their childhood, but Small Films output resists mere nostalgia. Although the animation may look slightly primitive, their charm has not been erased by the passing of time.

At the same time, TV was swimming with cartoons (before they were all corralled off into Cartoon Network): Tom and Jerry, Bugs Bunny, Daffy Duck, Scooby-Doo, Barney Bear. Plus there was *The Wonderful World of Disney* (which usually showed live-action, but occasionally would run some of the cheaper, shorter animation) and *Disney Time* every Easter and Christmas wherein someone would present a selection of clips from the bigger Disney features. Which, over time, saved you the bother of actually having to see the films at the cinema. However, it was at the cinema, aged four, that I was traumatised by *Pinocchio*, on re-release with *Old Yeller*. After witnessing Old Yeller being taken out to a barn and shot, I was in no fit state to watch small boys morphing into donkeys. I have to admit that I never really took to Mickey, Donald or Goofy; compared with Bugs and Daffy they seemed bland and (whisper it) not very funny. The only other Disney film that I took to as a child was *The Jungle Book*, but then I was in the cubs.

I was keener to see the latest Ray Harryhausen film, *The Golden Voyage of Sinbad* and *Sinbad and the Eye of the Tiger*, a whole cinema full of children waiting patiently for the actors to shut up and the next monster to put in an appearance. It was sobering to see an interview with the great man on *Clapperboard* (a long-defunct children's programme about film) and realise that his work was created in a small workshop, long after the film's actors and crew had departed to their next project. Still being a (big) kid, I was at the front of the queue for *Jurassic Park*, the implied message to viewers being: 'Roll up! Come and see the living, breathing dinosaurs'. The whole cinema was full of slightly bigger children waiting for the actors to shut up and the next monster to put in an appearance.

But enough of memory lane. The older I got and the more animation I saw, the more I realised how impressive the variety on display was. A dedicated animator can, by a process of what could be called alchemy, bring any object to life, no matter how dead or still. It's never just been a matter of line drawings versus computer pixels. There is sand on glass in Caroline Leaf's *The Owl Who Married a Goose*, glass figurines in Karel Zeman's *Inspirace*, bones and meat in Švankmajer's *Alice* . . . Likewise, it's never just been a case of, as a good friend of mine puts it so aptly, 'small things hitting each other'. There has been film noir parody in Aardman's *The Big Picture*, psychological horror in UPA's *The Tell-Tale Heart*, journeys of self-discovery such as Alison De Vere's *The Black Dog*, explorations of sexuality (from the erotic to the downright smutty) in Marv Newland's *Pink Komkommer*. In Lejf Marcussen's *Den Offentlige Røst*, we take a disturbing journey through a twilight world of art, discovering the Mona Lisa hidden in Bosch's *The Garden of Earthly Delights*. In Zdenko Gasparovic's *Satiemania*, Erik Satie's piano music links images of bored, naked women, men being bludgeoned left, right and centre, and boats in the rain. Its artwork is somewhere between George Grosz and Robert Crumb. Geoff Dunbar's *Ubu* brings Alfred Jarry's characters to rude life. And yet, many people still think of animation as kid's stuff.

One could blame Disney; many do. The standard that Disney set for animation: artistic but never 'art', the cinema-going public accepted as 'family entertainment' and Disney's besting of the competition meant that his was the dominant voice in the animation field. Consequently, anyone working to produce anything more challenging never really got a look in. Animation, unless people are determined to look deeper, still resides in that position. Despite knowing references to bullet-time video in *Shrek* or *The Blair Witch Project* in *Jimmy Neutron Boy Genius*, these remain 'family entertainment', the references placed as sops to the cine-literate adults in the audience to stop them getting restless. Animation for the 'family' is still the area of the industry that continues to draw most financing, simply because it's the area that pulls in high figures, both in box office and residuals, and specifically in marketing tie-ins. Nowadays, animated features aimed at an exclusively adult audience tend to reside in the 'art cinema' bracket: Jan Švankmajer, Richard Linklater and Bob Sabiston's *Waking Life* and Sylvain Choumet's *Belleville Rendez-vous*. While Hayao Miyazaki's *Spirited Away* was dubbed by Disney for Western markets, the distributors were canny enough to release a subtitled version as well. However, this bracketing could be seen as an improvement on the previous interpretation of 'adult' animation in juvenile outings like *Jungle Burger* and *Heavy Metal*.

This is not to suggest that all family-oriented animation has nothing to recommend it to 'mature' viewers. Two examples that spring to mind (and there are plenty more) are: *Tim Burton's The Nightmare Before Christmas*, with its echoes of Charles Addams and Edward Gorey, and Robert Zemeckis' and Richard Williams' *Who Framed Roger Rabbit?* which mixed live-action noir with reality-bending cartoons.

Roger Rabbit is an interesting example. While it uses many characters from animation's 'golden age' (Mickey Mouse, Bugs Bunny, Betty Boop, etc.), its setting is 1947, after the genre's boundaries had been limited by the Hays Code. Formally implemented in 1934 and not finally scrapped until 1968, the Hays Code set strict moral guidelines for filmmakers and clamped down on, amongst other things, the overt sexuality of Betty Boop. In *Roger Rabbit* she is presented as a washed-up black-and-white cartoon working as a cigarette girl. But 1947 was still a time when people went to see the latest Disney movie because it was an event, rather than just a feature-length advert to promote Happy Meal figurines. (Indeed, Disney's *Snow White* was restricted in Britain by the censorship authorities because it was felt that the witch was too frightening for children.) So, the opening Roger Rabbit/Baby Herman cartoon, a homage to the carnage-wreaking slapstick of Tex Avery, is particularly apposite, for the humour in Avery's cartoons was deliberately sophisticated. He had adopted this approach to target an audience for Warners that he felt Disney weren't catering for. By 1947, he had moved to MGM where he was producing his most *risqué* work.

Watching *Roger Rabbit* with some knowledge of the enmity between Disney and Warners, one realises that such battles never end, especially in these days of monolithic media corporations. Neither studio would allow their most iconic cartoon stars to appear in the film unless, like political broadcasts, they had equal time. And so, there are two carefully constructed scenes. In the first, Bob Hoskins' private eye, Eddie Valiant, goes to a night-club. On stage, playing a piano each, like the McGarrigle sisters, are two ducks, Donald and Daffy, getting equal time. Later, as Valiant plummets from a very tall building (after being chased by a combination of a Basil Wolverton grotesque and Avery's Minnie Hotcha! from *Big Heel-Watha*), he is met by two skydivers. They are Mickey Mouse and Bugs Bunny, who trade compliments before Bugs hands Valiant an anvil. Without being flippant, it is the cartoon equivalent of De Niro and Pacino meeting for coffee in Michael Mann's *Heat*.

The reception that Disney films garnered in the 1930s and 40s is currently being echoed in the box office records being broken by Pixar's output. Feature-length computer animation (Computer Generated Images or CGI) is still in its infancy and Pixar are ensuring that all ages are embraced by their films. The fact that their latest, *Finding Nemo*, was even more successful at the box-office than *Toy Story* suggests that this is not just down to novelty. How much attendances are down to the chilling 'pester-power' is another matter. While not choosing 'timeless' fairy tales, like Walt employed to appeal to a broad audience, Pixar go for timeless universal themes: the discarding of old toys in *Toy Story*, the scary creatures under the bed in *Monsters, Inc.*, the rites of passage in *Finding Nemo* and so on. It cannot be mere accident that the name 'Nemo' crops up in their latest. Not only does it reference one of Disney's more popular live-action features, *20,000 Leagues under the Sea* (1954) (based on the novel by Jules Verne, one of the founders of speculative fiction whose work inspired the first great special effects director, Georges Méliès) but also *Little Nemo in Slumberland*, the comic strip and first animated film by animation pioneer Winsor McCay. Extra resonance is conveyed when one realises that the Disney's *20,000 Leagues* was directed by Richard Fleischer, son of Walt's only major competitor in animation in the 1930s, Max Fleischer.

Pixar's attention to detail not only proves they have a team of dedicated animators, but also animators who are cine-literate to a point beyond mere pop-culture references. In *Toy Story*, the mutilated toys made by Sid, the evil kid next door, echo many of Jan Švankmajer's and the Quay Brothers' creations, and there's even a sly nod to Kubrick's *The Shining*: the carpet in Sid's house is the same as in the Overlook Hotel.

The advances of CGI are interesting, for surely its final

goal will be convincing replication of reality. It appears that Pixar and PDI, among others, with their conquering of new textures and environments with each movie, must be striving towards that goal. If this is achieved then CGI surely must leave the field of animation behind, at least in genre terms, and head towards live-action. CGI has already been used not just to create believable monsters but to bend reality (e.g. an actor's healthy legs digitally removed to make him an amputee in *Forrest Gump*, John Goodman's right-handed baseball playing altered to make him a southpaw in *Babe*), so why not a feature-length film featuring CGI-animated actors? Such scare stories have been around for a while: Marilyn Monroe and James Dean digitally resurrected and so on, but it has already happened to a certain degree. In Ridley Scott's *Gladiator* Oliver Reed's scenes were digitally created after the actor died during filming. Once animation reaches the level of perfectly replicating reality then it surely ceases to be animation as a genre. For, if there can be one general reason for the continuing appeal of animation, it is because, like fantasy literature, it presents us with the convincing evocation of a world that we know doesn't exist, but its believable representation on screen (whether talking animals or whole worlds) allows us to suspend our disbelief and immerse ourselves in it. If we wish to immerse ourselves in the real world then we can go and see a Ken Loach movie, or just step outside of our front door.

Likewise, the aim of this book is to present readers with the best of those who have created such worlds. It's only fair for me to point out that it might not be what you expected. It's not a history of animation. Well, it is, but not a *complete* history of animation. I would hope that this is fairly obvious, given how wee this book is in comparison with, say, Giannalberto Bendazzi's *Cartoons*, which is 514 pages long and already nearly ten years out of date. It bears repeating: I have had to leave a lot of people out, in some places entire continents, simply for reasons of concision and space. What I've tried to do is include people whose works might be more available to the interested reader. This doesn't mean that it's all available, simply that examples of their work are more likely to turn up on TV or in DVD/video racks than others. I've also tried to include some animators whose techniques differ from traditional methods in order to give an idea of how broad a church animation truly is. A lot of the choices are self-indulgent because they're personal favourites. So ultimately this book contains brief résumés of a mere handful of animators. But as Pocket Essentials are introductions above all, contained within are animators worth knowing about, particularly if you have a healthy curiosity about the subject.

I apologise for those I have had to omit, particularly Bill Plympton, Paul Terry, Paul Grimault, Walter Lantz, Terry Gilliam, Richard Williams, Len Lye, Frédéric Back, George Pal, Ray Harryhausen, Willis O'Brien, many anime directors, Otto Messmer, John and Faith Hubley, John Halas and Joy Batchelor, Bruno Bozzetto and many of the Warners directors amongst others. But I believe that those I have included are among the best the genre has produced, people who can breathe life into objects that never truly had life in the first place, whether they are ink on cels, sand on glass, lumps of Plasticine or pixels on a screen. I hope their worlds entrance you as much as they have me.

Pioneers

'Animation should be an art, that is how I conceived it. But as I see what you fellows have done with it is make it into a trade . . . not an art, but a trade . . . bad luck.'

Winsor McCay

Moments In
The Early History of Animation

1824 – Peter Mark Roget, a doctor at the University of London (and later creator of the Thesaurus) wrote the paper *Persistence of Vision with Regard to Moving Objects*. In this he noted that the retina retains images for a fraction of a second before the next image succeeds it. If the images were rapid enough, the viewer saw movement even though the pictures were still.

1825 – Physician John A Paris creates the thaumatrope, which is a disc with an image on each side with strings attached at the ends of the horizontal axis. As the disc is spun, the images appear to merge. For example, a bird on one side, a cage on the other. The disc is spun and the bird appears 'inside' the cage.

1832 – Belgian scientist Joseph Plateau creates the phenakistiscope. This is a pivot with a cardboard disc.

Successive images of an object in motion are drawn around the outside edge of the disc. The viewer watches the disc through a slit as it spins on the pivot. The object appears to move. Other variations on this idea followed, with various faux-Greek names.

1872 – French inventor and photographer's assistant Emile Reynaud builds the praxinoscope. It consists of a cylindrical box on a pivot. A coloured strip inside the box shows successive images of a movement. The box is rotated and the images reflected on a mirrored prism placed atop the pivot. Reynaud patented the gadget in 1877 and sold it as a children's toy.

1889 – Reynaud patents the *théâtre optique*. It is the praxinoscope modified to become a mass entertainment device. A projector and more mirrors had been added to show the films onto a screen. The images are now painted onto a long ribbon running between two spools. Another magic lantern projects background scenery onto the screen. His first film *Un Don Bock* (*A Good Beer*) is privately shown to friends. The machine's main drawback is that it has to be turned manually by an operator aware of all the necessary cues for rewinds, acoustical effects, etc. This complexity cools most buyers' enthusiasm and Reynaud's hopes of franchising the machine fall through.

1892 – Reynaud signs with the Grévin Museum for daily performances and a new programme every year. A clause in the contract prohibits sale of the praxinoscope or its films. Thus tied, Reynaud premieres his work on 28 October.

The shows remained popular up until 1900 when they ceased. But the Lumières' historic projection in 1895 marks the beginning of the end. Reynaud added improvements but, unwilling to produce films like the Lumières, he was soon left behind. His hand-painted films were no match for cinema's increasingly industrial approach. Depressed by his lack of advancement, Reynaud destroys the three *théâtre optiques* and throws his films in the Seine.

1895 – With the Lumières and Edison's instruments adopted as standards by the movie industry, research into optical equipment drops off. In August 1895 Alfred Clark, a cameraman for Edison, becomes arguably the first person to realise the potential of stopping cranking the camera in order to effect a change on screen. He uses this technique on *The Execution of Mary, Queen of Scots* to replace the actress about to be executed with a puppet.

1899 – Probably the first fully animated film is made by Arthur Melbourne. *Matches: An Appeal* uses animated matches to appeal to the British public to donate matches to the soldiers fighting in the Boer War.

1900 – James Stuart Blackton modifies drawings during a pause in camera-cranking for *The Enchanted Drawing*. This method is not strictly animation but one of several camera tricks (such as under- and over-cranking) that were mastered by users of this infant technology. Blackton had emigrated from Sheffield to the US aged ten. He was later hired by Edison on the strength of his abilities as a 'lightning sketch-artist' and was soon working as a cameraman, director and producer.

1906 – Blackton's hand appears on screen to draw the characters in his celebrated animation *Humorous Phases of Funny Faces*. Its highlight is a man blowing cigar smoke into a woman's face.

1907 – Blackton uses early stop-motion techniques to provide supernatural effects for his live-action film *The Haunted Hotel*. The film proves so successful that many studios seek to reverse-engineer his effects in order to reproduce them in their own films. The most important of these people as far as the evolution of the animated film is concerned is Emile Cohl.

Emile Cohl

He was born Emile Courtet in Paris in 1857. He had worked as a jeweller's apprentice and a magician's assistant before joining the army. It was here that he discovered his artistic abilities when he sketched many of his regiment. After demob he studied with artist André Gill and changed his name to Cohl, believing it sounded more exotic.

He became increasingly multi-faceted. He worked as a caricaturist for several magazines, wrote comedy plays and had a deep interest in magic tricks. In the 1880s he became proficient in photography. In 1907, so the story goes, Cohl was hired by Gaumont studio after confronting head honcho Leon Gaumont about plagiarizing one of his comedies. Gaumont, along with Pathé, dominated film production and distribution in France during the silent era.

At Gaumont, his abilities soon overtook those of James Blackton. Whereas Blackton insisted on retaining the real world in his animations, Cohl embraced the cartoon aspects wholeheartedly. His first film, a four-minute animation with autonomous characters entitled *Fantasmagorie* premiered on 17 August 1908. By the end of 1923, by his own count, he had made over 300 films. This figure may not include the many live-action shorts and special effects comedies that he also worked on. This period of remarkable activity marks his most creatively fertile period. It saw him lay out many of the tropes of animated films still used today. Characters destroy and recreate themselves, they metamorphose and are killed without spilling blood; they are devoured by surreal monsters and emerge unscathed. As well as cartoons, he also animated puppets and household objects and even painted colours directly onto the celluloid.

In 1912, having already left Gaumont and worked briefly for Pathé, Cohl went to work for the American branch of the Éclair company, based in Fort Lee. Here he worked on an animated version of Don McManus' strip cartoon *Snookums*. At first, Cohl was impressed with the well-established team and their rapport, as well as the producer's generous payments to the artists. Later, his opinion darkened as he discovered how American studios were using their mass-production techniques to make movies for overseas markets in a way that would crush opposition from independent filmmakers.

In March 1914, Cohl returned to Paris. During the First World War he made propaganda films and worked on another comic strip adaptation. By now, his creativity was waning and he spent the post-war period making mainly scientific films and adverts. Cohl died in 1938.

At around the same time as Cohl was leaving Gaumont, another artist across the Atlantic was making his first venture into animation.

Winsor McCay

Details of McCay's early life are now long lost, but it is thought that he was born around 1867 in Ontario. As a child, he was a compulsive drawer – rendering pictures with great accuracy and rapidity, characteristics that he would carry over into adulthood. Although his father tried to send him to business school, McCay spent much of the next few years working as a lightning artist and poster designer for various 'dime museums' (an enterprise containing many circus and sideshow elements, especially a freak show, pioneered by P T Barnum).

His experience at the dime museums proved far better training for his later career than formal art classes. His ability to render the human form not only in incredible variety and extremity but also in action proved essential to his work in strip cartoons and particularly in animation.

As his reputation as a lightning artist continued to grow, he was hired by the *Cincinnati Commercial Tribune* to draw pictures of 'freaks'. In 1898, he was given full-time employment at the *Tribune* drawing illustrations for the news before photography in newspapers had become widespread. He spent two years there before being head-hunted by the *Cincinnati Enquirer* for more pay. Still moonlighting, he also worked as a cartoonist for *Life* magazine.

He had already begun to create comic strips while at the *Enquirer* but in 1904 he went to work for the *New York Herald* and the *Evening Telegram*. Along with several short-lived strips, it was at the *Telegram* that he created *Dreams of the Rarebit Fiend*, whose popularity would only be eclipsed by the strip that he created in 1905: *Little Nemo in*

Slumberland. Rarebit Fiend invariably followed the same plot each strip. A character would have the most vivid and surreal nightmares. In the final frame he/she would awaken and blame it upon something he/she had eaten, usually a rarebit. While the story was the same, the dreams themselves were flights of beautifully rendered imagination. It was transferred to the *Herald* in 1911 and only closed in 1913.

Little Nemo started in the *Herald* in October 1905 and continued until 1911, when McCay went to work for Hearst. Like *Rarebit Fiend*, its story showed Little Nemo visiting Slumberland and having wild adventures for most of the strip, only for him to awaken in the final frame. Again, however, it was McCay's endlessly imaginative and beautifully drawn vision of Slumberland that gave the strip its appeal. Its popularity with the public was immediate and countless merchandising deals were struck during the strip's run. It was even adapted as a Broadway musical in 1908. When McCay went to work for Hearst, *Nemo* was retitled *The Land of Wonderful Dreams* and ran until 1914 in the *New York American*. A brief revival occurred in 1924–27, but McCay failed to recapture its former glory.

Little Nemo's termination came not so much from McCay but from Hearst. The press baron made it clear that he had hired McCay to draw editorial cartoons and other, less fanciful, work. McCay's financial situation (he had a wife and family to support) meant that he had to do what he was told, even though it meant the end of his work in cartoon strips.

From 1906, McCay had also had a flourishing part-time career in vaudeville as a lightning-sketch artist with an entertaining patter. When he began to explore animation, the results became part of the show also. His first short, made in 1911, was *Little Nemo*. It was primarily a demonstration of what was possible from animation. Much of the running time (ten and a half minutes) was live action footage of McCay betting friends that he can produce 4000 drawings in a month and make a motion picture from them. This he does. The animation was also hand-coloured and shows characters from *Little Nemo in Slumberland* bowing and changing shape. One character draws another and the two exit the screen in a dragon's mouth.

His next film, *How a Mosquito Operates* (1912), was an adaptation of an episode of *Rarebit Fiend* and showed a mosquito in a top hat draining a sleeping victim's blood. After one drink too many, the creature exploded. In 1914, McCay premiered his most memorable work in Chicago. *Gertie the Dinosaur* warmed up with live action footage of McCay and a friend visiting a dinosaur's skeleton in a museum. Here McCay bets that he can 'make the dinosaurus live again' via cartoons. Six months and 10,000 drawings later, he proves just that. The footage took up about five minutes out of the film's twelve and a half minutes running time. During this time, with McCay on stage acting as a ringmaster, Gertie performs several tricks for the audience. She also eats a tree, gets into a contretemps with a mammoth, does a little dance, gets thirsty and drains a lake and scratches her head with her tail. At the climax, she lifts a live action McCay onto her back and gallumphs off-screen with him. At the time, the notion of an animated character (a creation with a personality that engaged the audience's sympathies) was a novel concept. It would soon become one of the overriding concerns of animation studios.

The public and the press were entranced by *Gertie*, and rave reviews followed. The only newspapers that ignored it were those owned by Hearst. He personally instructed that there should be no mention of the event, nor any adverts carried for its performance. Hearst also carpeted McCay, telling him that his extracurricular activities should end and that he should concentrate on his full-time job at the *New York American*. As always, concerned about his income, McCay complied, and ceased his vaudeville performances.

Later, in 1917, while McCay was putting the finishing touches to his next film, Hearst again laid down the law. The film, *The Sinking of the Lusitania* (1918) was the result of 25,000 drawings, McCays most ambitious work and his most dramatic. Based on the wartime torpedoing of the British passenger ship by a German submarine, McCay's outrage propelled the movie. A brief live action introduction showed him settling down to create the drawings and there was a propagandistic passage where photographs of some of the more famous dead were shown. But McCay's artwork really has no need of these sections, for it conveys, with remarkable detail and passion, the full horror of the attack and the passengers' struggle to survive.

Despite Hearst's efforts, McCay did not entirely cease making animated films until 1921, and he was allowed some small reprieves to tour, mainly between 1922–25. But Hearst had spoken and, once again, managed to short-sightedly end a career in which McCay had demonstrated an individual genius. Mostly only fragments remain of his other films but of these, the three shorts based on *Dreams of a Rarebit Fiend* (*The Pet*, *The Flying House* and *Bug Vaudeville*, all 1921) show that he remained increasingly ambitious – each film runs to nearly 'featurette' length (12.5, 16 and 13.5 minutes respectively) and contain sequences of remarkable visual inventiveness.

Although it seems that Hearst put paid to McCay's continuing career as an animator, it can also be suggested that McCay saw the writing on the wall as far as animation was concerned. Despite being a showman at heart, he saw in animation the potential of a new fine art; something that he had personally realised in *The Sinking of the Lusitania*. But he could see that those following him into the field were content to mainly churn out cheap gags in cynical films that aspired to nothing greater than a healthy profit. Another possibility was that, like Reynaud before him, other animators' technical abilities were beginning to outstrip his own. Whatever the justification for him leaving the field, his contributions to the cartoon strip and animation cannot be underestimated. When he died in 1934, telegrams poured in to his family, not just from friends and colleagues but also from many fans who only knew him through his work.

Innovators

'Gee, this'll make Beethoven'
Walt Disney, viewing the rushes for the
Pastoral section of Fantasia.

Lotte Reiniger

Anyone who is familiar with the work of illustrator Jan
Pieńkowski (*Haunted House*, *A Necklace of Raindrops*) will
understand quite how magical silhouette illustrations can
be. Lotte Reiniger's name is synonymous with silhouette
animation; a form woefully under-explored in the field –
with, perhaps, the exception of Phil Mulloy's *Cowboys*
series (1991), which takes a more violent and scatological
approach.

Born Charlotte Reiniger in 1899, she was drawn to the
field of animation after attending a lecture on trick
photography given by Paul Wegener, a leading German
actor of the time. Wegener was a member of Max
Reinhardt's theatre company and Reiniger joined the
acting school attached to the company. To draw attention
to her abilities, she began to fashion silhouette figures of
many of the company's stars in their most famous roles.
Impressed, Wegener commissioned her to design the

captions for *The Pied Piper of Hamelin* (*Der Rottenfänger Von Hamelin*, 1918). In 1919, he introduced her to a fledgling experimental animation group, suggesting that they animate her silhouettes. The first movie, *The Ornament of the Lovestruck Heart* (*Das Ornament Des Verliebten Herzens*, 1919) received a positive enough public reception for her to continue making animated shorts – totalling over 50 by the time of her death.

In 1923, a banker named Louis Hagen presented her with a custom-built studio above his garage and the finance necessary to produce a feature-length film of her work. Along with her husband, Carl Koch, and Berthold Bartosch (both members of the animation group) and Walter Ruttmann who painted the backgrounds, Reiniger began work on *The Adventures of Prince Achmed* (*Die Abenteuer Des Prinzen Achmed*, 1926). Despite claims for Disney's *Snow White and the Seven Dwarfs* (1937), *Achmed* was the first genuinely feature-length animated movie. Mixing together several of the *Tales from 1001 Nights*, *Achmed* was filmed in black and white and then hand-tinted. It featured wax and sand animation as well as silhouettes, occasionally making use of a multiplane camera. On its initial release in 1926, *Achmed* had an over-whelmingly positive reception, winning support from several important directors including René Clair and Jean Renoir.

It was believed that all prints of *Achmed* were destroyed during the 1945 Allied bombing of Berlin but a black-and-white print was discovered in the BFI archives in 1956. Using Reiniger's original colouring instructions, the print was gradually restored and completed in 1970. Due to the difference in projection speeds (at the time of creation, they ran at 18 frames a second, whereas now it is 24 frames), the 90 minute feature shrank to about 65 minutes. A new, reportedly inferior score, written by Freddie Phillips, was added to replace the lost original created by Wolfgang Zeller. Another loss was much of Ruttmann's finer background detailing.

Reiniger followed up *Achmed*'s success with a second feature in 1928, this time based upon the stories of Hugh Lofting and entitled *Dr Dolittle and his Animals* (*Doktor Dolittle Und Seine Tiere*). Its score was written by Paul Dessau, Paul Hindemith and Kurt Weill. The version that remains again has an inferior new score and again runs at an accelerated speed. By the time of its original release, the film was hindered by the fact that talking pictures had risen to dominance.

Two later features also met with problems. The first, an adaptation of Ravel's *L'Enfants et Les Sortilèges* (*The Child and the Witcheries*, 1925) with a libretto by Colette, stalled due to copyright problems. A second, live-action feature that Reiniger co-directed: *The Pursuit of Happiness* (*Die Jagd Nach Dem Glück,* 1929), which starred Jean Renoir and Berthold Bartosch, was, like *Doctor Dolittle*, hamstrung by being a silent film when audiences were clamouring for talkies. An attempt to dub in dialogue was unsuccessful.

With the Nazis rising in influence, Reiniger and Koch realised that they were under threat. Their attempts to leave the country were frustrated by several other governments (including Britain and France) refusing them visas. Reiniger continued to make films, several containing hidden anti-Nazi messages. They finally managed to leave

Germany by piggy-backing on a succession of temporary visas. Renoir helped the couple out wherever possible by employing them on his own films. When war did break out, he took them to Italy where he was directing *Tosca* (1941), a task which he handed over to Koch. The couple stayed in Italy until 1944 when the Allied advance forced them to return to Germany. Once there, Reiniger started on the unfinished *The Goose that Laid the Golden Eggs* (*Die Goldene Gans*).

They were finally allowed to leave Germany in 1948. They moved to Britain, founding Primrose Productions. Exhausted by the war, Koch died not long afterwards, but Reiniger lived to a ripe old age, producing silhouette animation for adverts and the BBC. Her last film, completed at 80, was *The Rose and the Ring* (1979) from the story by Thackeray. During this period, she also produced work with the National Film Board of Canada, including *Aucassin and Nicolette* (1975). She died in Germany in 1981.

The Fleischers

The story of the Fleischer brothers and their contribution to animation is one of innovation, struggle, success and good old-fashioned sibling rivalry. There were seven children in the Fleischer family, but the four who became involved in the fledgling animation industry were Max (born 1883), Joe (1889), Lou (1891) and Dave (1894), but Max and Dave were the real creative force.

Born in the US of Austrian-emigrant parents, the Fleischer brothers all seem to have inherited their father's flair for inventing. Both Max and Dave showed an artistic streak from an early age. After a varied education, Max became a staff artist for Brooklyn's *Daily Eagle*. Here he became friends with soon-to-be animation pioneer, John Randolph Bray. After leaving the *Eagle*, Max eventually became art editor at *Popular Science Magazine*. During this time he realised that animation would marry his twin interests.

Nine years younger, Dave had worked for some time as an usher at the Palace Theater where he studied the performances of the vaudeville entertainers. After a spell in the art department of an engraving company, he became a film cutter at Pathé Films in 1912.

In 1911, inspired by Winsor McCay's *Little Nemo* film, several would-be animators (including Bray) began working on ways to lighten an animator's workload. Meanwhile, Max worked on an invention to reduce the need for artistry in animation. Named the rotoscope, it helped revolutionise animation. With it, sequences to be animated could be filmed in live action and then blown-up frames would be traced and painted over to turn them into animated pictures. It also reduced much of the jerkiness that was a problem with animation at the time. Max patented it in 1917, although a company in Pennsylvania had been using a similar device before him and Disney would use something similar for much of the 'human' animation in *Snow White*.

Joe constructed the rotoscope using a drawing board with a frosted-glass centre. A movie projector shone one frame at a time onto the glass. Max then drew the pictures using tracing paper. Their live action star was Dave, dressed as a clown, running through vaudeville routines.

This gave the brothers their first Ko-Ko the Clown film. It took them about a year to complete at a length of a mere 100 feet. In it, the artist's hand drew Ko-Ko onto paper, the little clown did some tricks then turned back into ink which dripped back into the inkwell. They took the film to Pathé, who laughed at the lengthy process. To speed things up, Max mixed live action footage in with the animation, reducing production to a month. Pathé accepted and requested a fifteen-minute long animation about the life of Theodore Roosevelt. Apparently, it was so bad, Pathé showed them the door again.

So Max hawked the Ko-Ko film around other studios. At Paramount he bumped into John Bray again. Bray had an exclusive contract at Paramount with his compilation of short films, *The Paramount-Bray Pictograph*, but he was interested in Max's animation and offered to include it in his compilation. The short, now titled *Out of the Inkwell* (1916) was a hit with audiences and Bray commissioned Max and Dave to produce one a month.

They started properly after the First World War, first for Bray at Paramount and then moving to Goldwyn with him. By this time, Dave was the director and scripter, Max the animator. Max's insistence on having sole credit caused several arguments. After one of these, Dave left the company, but things were eventually smoothed over and he returned. In 1921, the pair formed Out of the Inkwell Films, Inc. in conjunction with Bray animator Charles Shettler, with Joe working as cameraman. Their small studio was successful enough to hire staff to do the drawing for them. Max then became the manager.

1923 saw them produce the live-action/animation film *The Einstein Theory of Relativity* and the more contentious *Darwin's Theory of Evolution*. Around the same time, song-writer Charles K Harris came to them with the idea of films that would encourage the audience to sing along with the cinema organist (this being before talkies). The brothers came up with the idea of a bouncing ball following the lyrics on screen, keeping the audience in time with the music. It was introduced in September 1925, with *My Bonnie (Lies over the Ocean)*. By then, several of the Ko-Ko Song Car-Tunes, as they were known, had been released *sans* ball, starting with *Oh Mabel* (1924). Ko-Ko would perform, followed by the song. An animated ball was later replaced by a live action one and the popular series continued until 1927. In the aftermath of *The Jazz Singer's* success, the brothers introduced Screen Songs, these were also ball-led singalongs but with a live action singer.

Although silent, their Song Car-Tunes had forced the Fleischers to consider synchronization well before most animators. Their backer, Hugo Riesenfeld, introduced them to radio-pioneer Lee De Forest who, in 1919, had patented the basic process for adding sound to movies. De Forest suggested sound cartoons and the Fleischers produced a few Song Car-Tunes with a basic soundtrack as musical backgrounds. Their *My Old Kentucky Home* (1926) was possibly the first sound cartoon. Max, however, didn't really see the idea catching on and so Disney stole a march on them.

Max's other major contribution to animation came around the same time. At that time, one animator would produce all of the drawings for a film. Eager to free up one of their better animators, Dick Huemer, for more important things, Max asked him to let a lowlier member of staff to fill in the bits between the 'key' positions in the animation. Dick agreed and so, it appears, was created the job of the 'in-betweener'. A brief example would be that a character takes a running jump. The key scenes would be a) the character at the beginning of the leap, and b) of him landing at the end. The in-between job would fill in the travelling from a to b.

By 1927, the Fleischers were contracted to Paramount following a couple of failed attempts to strike out independently. 1929 saw the first in their Screen Songs: *The Sidewalks of New York* – their attempt to rival *Steamboat Willie. Noah's Lark* (also 1929) launched their Talkartoons, taking on Disney's Silly Symphonies. Brother Lou helped to synchronise the sound, which was added to the completed animation. With Ko-Ko having been retired in 1927 with *Koko Needles the Boss*, the brothers took his dog, Fitz, renamed him Bimbo and made him the star of the Talkartoons. His star was soon to wane, though. In the cartoon *Dizzy Dishes* (1930), animator Grim Natwick gave Bimbo a female companion. Although she had enough doggy behaviour to appeal to Bimbo, she also had attributes that would appeal to male humans in the audience. She wasn't given a name until *Stopping the Show* (1932), but anyone seeing *Dizzy Dishes* today would instantly recognise Betty Boop.

She was popular right from her first starring vehicle *Silly Scandals* (1931) until her retirement in mid-1939. With Bimbo and a resurrected Ko-Ko as sidekicks, the

Fleischers produced more than one Betty cartoon a month. Dave redesigned her to lose those worrisome canine attributes. With huge eyes and a bigger head, a lot of cleavage, and skirts increasingly shorter, revealing a gartered leg, she coupled a childlike innocence with a big sexual charge. In *Betty Boop's Rise to Fame* (1934) she even flashed a breast (a while back, an enterprising archivist slowed down some Betty footage and found far stronger stuff slipped into the occasional subliminal frame). She was voiced most memorably by May Questel and modelled on actress/singer Helen Kane. In 1934, Kane sued the Fleischers for plagiarism, thereby damaging her popularity as the public now believed that she was copying Betty. The Fleischers told several whoppers during their defence and the case was thrown out of court. Betty isn't the only thing to enjoy about her cartoons, however. Dave Fleischer's continuing fascination with the alchemical transmutations that animation can cause is in full flourish in these films, as well as an obsession with ghosts and monsters, usually full of both lust and menace. The popping soundtracks, the chases, the sexuality, the gentle swaying of Betty to popular jazz tunes of the day and the weird metamorphoses going on around her, combine to give the films an eerie, dream-like quality.

Sadly, her career was destroyed by the censorious Hays Code of 1934, charged with cleaning up Hollywood's output. From 1935, Betty's sexuality was dramatically toned down, her storylines became increasingly bland. She didn't even bother to turn up for her last advertised short *Yip Yip Yippy* (1939).

Helping to fill the void that Betty had left was Popeye

the Sailor. Max had bought the screen rights to E C Segar's strip a few years before. He had been introduced in the eponymous Betty Boop cartoon of 1933 and soon became mystifyingly popular. Although Dave Fleischer's inventive input was a lot lower on the Popeye cartoons, the brothers did get Segar to make some changes. Popeye's adversary, Bluto, was created for the films, and much greater emphasis was placed upon the sailor's spinach-habit. Popeye's popularity meant that the Fleischers produced hundreds of shorts up until 1957, as well as three feature-films.

During this time, they extended their Color Classics series, begun in 1934. The most notable was Betty Boop's colour debut *Poor Cinderella* (1934), which featured an innovative 3-D process of filming the animation over a model set. While they had produced their own version of *Snow White* in 1933 (starring Betty), their calculated response to Disney's 1937 version was an adaptation of the Lilliput segment of *Gulliver's Travels*. Unfortunately, it was terribly dull. Their attempts to spin off some of the characters from the movie were equally unsuccessful.

The Fleischers' second, and last, attempt at feature-length animation, *Hoppity Goes to Town* (1941) was markedly better. For anyone who has seen Dreamworks' *Antz* (1998) or Pixar's *A Bug's Life* (1998), the plot holds few surprises: A grasshopper attempts to save his threatened community of bugs from human intrusion and predatory villainous insects. It benefited from plenty of action and excellent characterization.

However, the film's success didn't save them from an approaching storm. Max had bought the screen rights to

Siegel and Schuster's *Superman*. The first instalment was released three months after *Hoppity*, using characters extensively rotoscoped for heightened realism. True to form, Max wanted sole credit. Dave bridled and the brothers had a final falling out. It came to light that during the filming of *Hoppity* Max had telegraphed Paramount refusing to work with Dave ever again. Paramount demanded early repayment of a huge loan on the Fleischer studio. When the brothers couldn't pay up, Paramount foreclosed and took many of Max's staff to set up their own animation wing, Famous Studios.

Meanwhile, Dave was snapped up by Columbia to head Screen Gems. Here he worked on *The Fox and the Crow* series (begun by Frank Tashlin in 1941) and animated shorts based on Al Capp's *Li'l Abner* strip. He soon departed for Universal where he wrote gags, worked on special effects and generally helped out on various projects including Hitchcock's *The Birds* (1963) and *Thoroughly Modern Millie* (1967). He died in 1979.

Max joined the James Handy Organization and made animated training films. It is reported that other members of staff were surprised by his poor animation technique. He produced Christmas-favourite *Rudolph the Red-Nosed Reindeer* (1944) and wrote the book *Noah's Shoes* (1944), a thinly-veiled attack on his brothers. In 1955, he sued Paramount when they televised Fleischer shorts with altered credits. The case was settled out of court. In 1958, he was appointed head of the art department at the J R Bray studio where he later tried to restart the *Out of the Inkwell* series. He died in 1972.

Joe worked for Famous Studios before quitting to

become an electrical contractor and died in 1979.

Lou made several bouncing ball training films for the army and then moved to California to become a piano teacher. He died in 1985.

Walt Disney

Born in Chicago on 5 December 1901, Walter Elias Disney is today still known as an animator. In fact, he never made animated films after 1924. He became interested in cartooning at an early age and, later, took a correspondence course in cartooning and attended night classes at the Art Institute of Chicago. In 1918, he faked his date of birth and enlisted in the American Ambulance Corps, spending a year in France. Back in Chicago, he got Christmas temp work at the Pesmen–Rubin Commercial Art Studio, alongside Ubbe Iwwerks (later to become Ub Iwerks). Sacked after the Christmas rush, they set up together as Iwerks–Disney Commercial Artists, a venture that lasted a few brief weeks. Getting work at the Kansas City Film Ad Company, Disney became convinced that he could make better animated features than the primitive stop-motion fare produced there.

In 1922, he set up Laugh-O-Gram Films with Iwerks and other young animators (including Rudolph Ising and Hugh Harman). They started by producing animated shorts based on traditional stories (such as *Jack and the Beanstalk*), as well as experimenting in various styles including clay stop-motion.

The studio was effectively killed off by a disastrous distribution deal. Although Laugh-O-Gram's days were numbered, Walt planned to film live action accompaniments for popular songs played by the organist from his local cinema, one Carl Stalling. Only one film was made but Stalling would become a popular composer for animated films.

The one item Walt saved from Laugh-O-Gram's creditors was *Alice's Wonderland*, the pilot for a new live-action/animation series. In July 1923, he touted it round Hollywood. At that time, the animation industry was based in New York; no Hollywood studio had an animation wing. In the meantime, he set up a primitive animation studio in his uncle's garage and tried unsuccessfully to get work as a live-action director.

Walt and *Alice* finally got a deal with New York distributor, Margaret Winkler. Walt's biggest outlay was the $100 a month contract to persuade his *Alice*, Virginia Davis (the live-action to Walt's animation) and her family to move to California. Winkler demanded the highest quality of *Alice* and Walt, knowing he wasn't a good enough animator to meet her standards, persuaded Ub Iwerks to come and work for him again. From *Alice Gets in Dutch* (1924) Iwerks made the films and Walt never animated again.

However, a few troubles arose when Winkler married distributor Charles Mintz: he took over her business and was much slower to pay up. He did contract Disney to produce 18 *Alice* shorts, which allowed Walt and brother Roy to take on more staff and buy a lot in Burbank. Mintz also arranged a deal between Disney Bros. Studio and Universal's Carl Laemmle, who needed a new cartoon star. Oswald the Lucky Rabbit's first film *Poor Papa* (released 1928) was turned down by Laemmle as the character was much too disreputable. A cleaned-up Oswald (uncannily resembling Otto Messmer's Felix the Cat) in *Trolley Troubles* (1927) won Disney the contract to produce a new cartoon every fortnight. However, when the year's contract was up, Mintz offered Walt a much lower deal. When Walt refused, Mintz pointed out the contract's terms; Universal owned the rights to Oswald. Further, Mintz was going to hire Walt's staff to continue the series, with or without him.

He carried out his threat and produced six Oswald cartoons before, satisfyingly, he was put out of business when Laemmle stepped in and handed the series to Walter Lantz (who would later find fame as the creator of the amusing but irritating Woody Woodpecker).

Taking the Mickey

Now comes a sizeable chunk of Disney mythology. The official story goes that, coming back from Mintz, Walt and wife Lillian dreamed up a new cartoon character. Walt called him Mortimer Mouse, Lillian told Walt to give him a less snobbish name. A more believable version is Iwerks told Walt and Roy that, if they doctored Oswald, they had a mouse and, more particularly, a 'new' character that wouldn't draw a lawsuit from Mintz and Universal. Disney Studios insists that Iwerks created Mickey's form, but Walt created his personality. This is a bit thick, if Mickey was only a hastily re-edited Oswald but, with the birth of 'talkies' Walt did give Mickey his personality, almost literally, as he voiced the character and acted out new story ideas to his animators.

For the first story, they drew on Lindbergh's recent

non-stop solo transatlantic flight. It had already inspired an Oswald cartoon (*The Ocean Hop*, 1927), so why not Mickey? And so, with the help of some barnyard animals, Mickey builds his aeroplane and takes Minnie along for the trip in *Plane Crazy* (1928). Contracted to produce three more Oswald cartoons and with many of the traitorous staff still working out their notice, even Walt realised that Mickey's debut had to remain completely secret. Allegedly, Iwerks completed over 600 drawings a day, with Lillian and Roy's wife, Edna, inking and painting. Walt then had the cels photographed by the one loyal cameraman. The silent *Plane Crazy* was previewed in May 1928. By Mickey's next outing, *Gallopin' Gaucho* (1928), the staff had departed, allowing Iwerks to call on help from the few remaining animators, including Les Clark and Wilfred Jackson, both of whom became highly respected Disney animators. With two Mickey shorts in the can, Walt tried out distributors. No one bit, feeling that they were good but undistinguished.

Despite *The Jazz Singer*'s impressive reception at its premiere on 6 October 1927, most senior Hollywood figures still felt that sound was a gimmick. However, Walt saw in it a way to distinguish Mickey's adventures. Rather than adding sound to the two existing shorts, he decided to make a third Mickey cartoon with sound, despite straitened finances. *Steamboat Willie* (1928) was partially inspired by Buster Keaton's recent silent hit *Steamboat Bill, Jr* and it was hoped the public might make a similar connection if all else failed.

Carl Stalling composed the soundtrack (incorporating two tunes that Walt had suggested) and the sound synchronisation was worked out from scratch using a metronome. Unable to afford RCA's sound system, Walt turned to the shady Pat Powers who offered him the Cinephone system, a cheaper, pirated version of RCA's set-up. With Walt voicing Mickey, they got a 'good' recording of the soundtrack out of the Cinephone sessions, although it nearly bankrupted them in the process.

Walt still found distributors hard to convince. He doorstepped independent cinema-owners and finally got lucky. Harry Reichenbach, the promoter for Colony Theater near Broadway, saw a big future for sound cartoons. He even paid Disney to give *Steamboat Willie* its first run. It premiered on 18 November 1928 and was better received that the main feature. Suddenly distributors became *very* interested but most of them wanted to buy Mickey as well as the films. After Oswald, there was no way Walt was losing another character. Realising that promoting Mickey meant promoting Cinephone, Powers offered Walt a tenyear licensing deal with several strings attached. Despite Roy's doubts, Walt took the deal.

In January 1930, the brothers paid Powers $100,000 to buy back Mickey's rights and exit the contract. Powers had embezzled over $150,000 royalties and took the deal. These amounts show just how successful Mickey was becoming. The next month, through Frank Capra, a new contract was arranged with Columbia. Disney would be paid $7,000 for each new cartoon. This arrangement lasted only two years, when Walt went to United Artists who doubled Columbia's amount.

Two months after *Steamboat Willie*'s success, bigger studios were producing their own sound cartoons.

Realising that novelty wasn't enough, Walt began casting around for other series to help keep Disney ahead of the competition. He also hired more animators. When Carl Stalling, now Disney's musical director, suggested an animated series that told their stories through music and visuals (thus avoiding still complex lip-synching), Walt took the chance. The series, *Silly Symphonies*, began with the Iwerks-animated *Skeleton Dance* (1929), a rare turn for the macabre.

It was just after *Skeleton Dance* that Iwerks left Disney, having become increasingly dissatisfied with Walt's habit of altering animators' work after close of shop. Believing quality drew greater rewards, Iwerks had irked Walt by creating all of *Skeleton Dance* himself. Walt felt his most experienced (and expensive) animator should be using in-betweeners and getting on with more important things. Iwerks signed with Powers and set up his own studio. Believing that Disney had lost its essence with Iwerks, Carl Stalling also left. He spent a short unhappy time with Paul Terry's studio before moving through various others, including Iwerks'.

In the early 1930s Walt and probably scripter Webb Smith introduced an important innovation to animation: the storyboard. While some animated features had been formally scripted, many (including those at Disney) had been made up by the animators as they went along. Storyboarding wasn't new to film directors (Méliès had used the idea intermittently, as had Alfred Hitchcock in the 1920s), but for animators it was a revelation. Enabling them to detail all key scenes and actions, it also gave animators the chance to reshuffle and edit scenes before any actual filming had begun.

Obviously, this facility for everyone to see what was planned and offer alternatives did not always benefit the film. John Kricfalusi's storyboards for *Ren and Stimpy* were famously torn to shreds on several occasions by Nickelodeon control-freaks, and a similar 'process' occurred with Oskar Fischinger's abstract designs for the *Toccata and Fugue* section of Disney's *Fantasia* (1940). But its introduction also allowed Walt to exploit his own particular talent as a storyteller and aid character development – both important elements in Disney's dominance over many of their competitors.

Finally making a profit, Disney expanded accordingly. From the six people employed in 1928, it had grown to 187 by 1934 (and over 1,600 by 1940). The studio also expanded to accommodate the growing workforce. Walt had originally wanted to hire New York's finest animators, but many of them shied away from his work ethic. Instead, the company hired beginners, putting them through an unofficial Disney school of art to train them in animation. The studio's method of production, a form of Taylorism, meant specialised teams dedicated to either animation, scene design, scripts, layouts or special effects. Inking, colouring and filming were also kept to separate teams. Walt himself stuck to organisation and motivation, handing out corrections and, less often, praise.

The other major advancement that Walt embraced was that of colour film. Other studios were put off by the cost and the Hollywood big shots believed colour to be a fad, like sound. Walt signed an exclusive contract with Technicolor in 1932 for two years. For their first colour outing, he selected the *Silly Symphonies*, *Trees and Flowers*. After several experiments, the animators found a paint that wouldn't peel from the acetate cels or fade under the powerful lights.

Colour rapidly improved the quality of the *Silly Symphonies*. One of them, *The Wise Little Hen* (1935) introduced Disney's second major character, the short-fused Donald Duck. By the appearance of the first colour Mickey Mouse short in 1935, Walt was already planning the company's most ambitious project yet. *Snow White and the Seven Dwarfs* (1937) partly originated from Walt's desire to be the first to make an animated feature film. Although, of course, outside the US, he had already been beaten both by the allegedly hour-long (no prints survive) Argentinian political satire *El Apóstol* (1917) animated by Quirino Cristiani; and definitively by Lotte Reiniger's *The Adventures of Prince Ahmed*. Walt's other reason was financial – while the animated shorts were successful, their costs were rising and revenue was slow to accumulate. Sooner or later, the two sums would cancel each other out. Planning began in 1934 and it wasn't long before Hollywood was buzzing. They called it 'Disney's Folly'. Even inside Disney there were concerns: both Roy and Lillian baulked at Walt's proposed budget of half a million dollars. His insistence on perfection meant the final cost was closer to one and a half million.

Adapted from the Grimm's fairy tale, *Snow White* contained all the right elements: innocence (Snow White) persecuted by evil (the wicked Queen), rescued by donor characters (the Dwarfs), further tribulations (poisoned by the Queen with an apple) and good finally triumphant through true love (the Queen killed by the Dwarfs, Snow White saved from death by a kiss from the handsome prince). Using such a timeless story was a canny idea, for the company were virtually breaking new ground. Great attention was paid to giving each character individuality and depth. The dwarfs in the Grimm story are just dwarfs – the dwarfs here are all memorable individuals, particularly due to Bill Tytla's animation and design. The colours of the film are carefully applied to each scene's mood and, in the reverse of the *Silly Symphonies*, the songs progress from the narrative (as with 'proper' musicals). Today Disney has a jaw-dropping ability to throw the word 'classic' at any product over a year old. *Snow White and the Seven Dwarfs* is, however, the one Disney film that rightfully deserves it.

Once *Snow White*'s success was ensured (it was critically and publicly well received), production went ahead on Disney's second feature, *Pinocchio* (1940). Despite its beautiful artwork and some superb characterization (including Bill Tytla's Stromboli), *Pinocchio* made a huge loss. Walt's insistence on perfection had its costs and the Second World War had virtually closed down all overseas markets. *Pinocchio* is also notable for its extensive use of the multiplane camera, developed by Ub Iwerks who had returned to Disney. The multiplane camera uses several background layers, each placed at a different distance from the camera-lens, to create an illusion of depth. Each layer except the furthermost have holes in their details so that the camera can 'see' through them. Whichever layer the camera focuses on means the others, consistent with our own vision, are slightly out of focus. As the camera-focus alters, we are given the illusion of moving through the scenery. However, the creation of all these separate backgrounds is not cheap, and *Pinocchio's* opening scene used twelve layers.

To recoup losses, Walt capitulated to requests to spin off characters from *Pinocchio* into short films (he had previously resisted with *Snow White*). It's a habit that continues at Disney to this day (for example Timon and Pumba from *The Lion King*).

In a further attempt to bring in more revenue, Walt struck on the idea of producing a feature film (financially more rewarding than short films) composed of short films (cheaper to produce than a feature). At that point, the studio was already working on a Mickey Mouse short based on Dukas' *The Sorcerer's Apprentice*. A chance encounter between Walt and conductor Leopold Stokowski led to *Fantasia* (1940). Perhaps the kindest thing that can be said about Walt's attempt to bring culture to the masses is that it's not as bad as *Fantasia 2000* (1999). Indeed, some of the sequences are very good indeed, particularly the enduring *Sorcerer's Apprentice* (the Mickey Mouse cartoon for people who don't like Mickey Mouse) and *Night on Bald Mountain* (unfortunately ruined by plonking *Ave Maria* on the end of it). The most unforgivable (although animated by *Pogo's* Walt Kelly) is Beethoven's *Pastoral* which gives us a My Little Pony version of Greek mythology – all syrup and no horse sweat.

To further help finances, Walt released *The Reluctant Dragon* (1941), a cheap compilation of animated shorts plus a Robert Benchley-hosted documentary. Audiences weren't impressed but the film's cheapness helped it turn a profit.

Meanwhile, unionization of the staff arrived in the form of the Screen Cartoonists Guild, headed by Herbert Sorrell. Sorrell and Walt were soon at loggerheads. When Walt sacked senior animator Art Babbitt as a troublemaker, Sorrell called a strike and half the animators walked out. It permanently damaged the studio and Walt's reputation, as he used the FBI and HUAC to persecute the strikers. With the studio at half-staff, *Dumbo* (1941) was pushed through, relying on pure animation and charm. It was an immediate success.

While Walt took a crew on a goodwill tour of South America, the strike was resolved. Most of the strikers were reinstated, but soon left for good, including Babbitt. Back at Disney, Walt set to getting *Bambi* (1942) completed. Where *Dumbo*'s animation was spare, *Bambi* was richly detailed with nature (for Disney) fairly red in tooth and claw. Bambi's mother's deftly handled death remains one of the great emotional moments of animation. Although successful, its huge cost again meant profits were that much smaller.

After *Bambi*, quality control began to slide. The South American junket had produced two compilation movies and 1946–48 saw several more, including *The Adventures of Ichabod and Mr Toad*, which tackled both Kenneth Grahame and Washington Irving. Disney also began to explore cheaper-per-foot live-action features. The studio's first fully live-action film was *Treasure Island* (1950).

Cinderella (1950) was Walt's return to feature-length animation, and showed that he had learned from his previous features. A classic fairy tale, like *Snow White*, it had beautifully rendered backgrounds like *Pinocchio* and, like *Dumbo*, the artwork was spare, letting story and characterization drive it.

Walt's attempts to tackle British children's classics were less successful. Of *Alice in Wonderland* (1951) and the later *The Sword in the Stone* (1963), the less said the better. If it's possible to say less than that, then it should be said about Disney's *Winnie the Pooh* adaptations which convinced at least one generation that Pooh was American. *Peter Pan* (1953) was better, but lost the dark undercurrents of J M Barrie's books.

He was on surer ground with *The Lady and the Tramp* (1955), which benefited from being made in Cinemascope, allowing the characters more room to manoeuvre. It was also an original story with no source material to betray. By now, Walt was becoming increasingly preoccupied with Disneyland which opened the same year. Much of the production responsibilities were handed to the studio's veterans, especially the 'Nine Old Men' (Milton Kahl, Marc Davis, Eric Larson, Wolfgang Reitherman, Les Clark, Ward Kimball, John Lounsbery, Frank Thomas and Ollie Johnston). Despite its critics, Disneyland's profits probably saved the studio which had taken another beating with the poor box-office reception of *Sleeping Beauty* (1959), which many considered as *Snow White* reheated.

As before, the next film, *One Hundred and One Dalmatians* (1961) was deliberately cheaper. Ub Iwerks helped matters by ingeniously adjusting a Xerox machine so that an animator's pencil drawings could be photocopied straight onto the cels, removing the need for inking. The problem was that everything had to have a firm black line, losing most drawings' subtleties. The animators of *Dalmatians* got round this by going for a far less naturalistic style. Helped by fast pacing and fine characterization, *Dalmatians* was very popular and, like the best of Disney's output, remains so.

Iwerks also worked on Walt's adaptation of *Mary Poppins* (1964), developing the travelling matte techniques that helped marry the live action and animated sequence. Despite Dick Van Dyke's execrable 'cockney' accent, *Mary Poppins* was a massive hit and made a major star of Julie Andrews.

Walt would supervise one last film, the boisterous *Jungle Book* (1967), which bore little relation to Kipling's original but has some of the more memorable songs and characters in the Disney canon — particularly George Saunders' turn as the suavely evil tiger Shere Khan. It was during that film's production that Walt was found to have lung cancer. Although the lung was surgically removed, Walt collapsed at home on 31 November 1966. He died on 15 December. Behind him, he left a monolithic entertainment corporation that, with a more conservative management, never again faced the same financial problems. While the corporation has become synonymous both with cultural hegemony and movies of a high saccharine content, Walt himself, while recoiling from art cinema, proved that entertainment could still be artistically made. While showing that feature animation could be a successful art form, to general audiences Disney also became the only standard for that art form.

Since his passing, the company has continued producing animated features in varying degrees of quality. Arguably the nadir was reached in late 70s/early 80s with films such as *Robin Hood* (1973) and *The Fox and the Hound* (1981). Many animators left in protest, including Don Bluth (who would go on to produce several features that would rival Disney for schmaltz) and Henry Selick and Tim Burton. The two would later reunite for the remarkable *Tim Burton's The Nightmare Before Christmas* (1993) (although Burton's early *Vincent* (1982) made at and shelved by Disney is also worth tracking down). In the 90s under Michael Eisner, Disney had a brief renaissance, with a string of hits including *Beauty and the Beast* (1991), *Aladdin* (1992) and *The Lion King* (1994). Its lucrative deal with Pixar (see chapter 7) has only served to shine a harsh light on the failure of some of Disney's more recent line animation, such as *Atlantis: The Lost Empire* (2001) and *Treasure Planet* (2002).

Broadening Horizons

'(Leon Schlesinger was a man whose) sole method of determining the quality of an animated cartoon was how far it came in under budget.'

Chuck Jones

Termite Terrace

After leaving Disney and then Mintz, Hugh Harman and Rudolf Ising went into business on their own. They came up with the character Bosko (not a stone's throw from Mickey Mouse) and marketed their first film *Bosko the Talk-Ink Kid*. The highest bidder was Leon Schlesinger, head of Pacific Art & Title and a distant relative of the Warner brothers. Schlesinger had helped finance Warners move to sound and used his good graces to get a distribution deal. Thus, he became the producer of their animated films. Mainly concerned with costs and deadlines, Schlesinger allowed his animators free rein on their creations. His hands-off approach helped to establish the group of artists for whom Warners Brothers cartoons remain justly famous.

In 1930, Harman and Ising began *Looney Tunes*, at this point a vehicle for Bosko and his friends, and *Merrie*

Melodies, a series mimicking Disney's *Silly Symphonies* featuring songs that Warners had used in their musicals. By 1933, they had left Warners, choosing MGM's distribution deal after Schlesinger had turned down a larger investment. They took Bosko with them, but during their brief stint at Warners they had produced 40 Bosko shorts.

After trying two ex-Disney directors, Jack King and Tom Palmer (both of whom he soon fired again), Schlesinger hired two newcomers, Tex Avery and Frank Tashlin. He also promoted Friz Freleng to a director.

Until Jack Warner closed the studio in 1957, the team that produced *Looney Tunes* and *Merrie Melodies* became synonymous with a particular style of anarchic cartoon – wise-cracking characters, endless chases, vast piles of TNT. While some characters can be pinned down to a single creator (such as Friz Freleng's alter ego Yosemite Sam), others evolved through several directors' cartoons and were very much a product of the team-working spirit at Warners. Bugs Bunny, Elmer Fudd, Daffy Duck, all gradually developed into the forms that we know them today. Bugs Bunny had already appeared in three cartoons before Tex Avery used him in *A Wild Hare* (1940) and he began to take on his recognisable characteristics. Elmer Fudd had started life as a character called Egghead. Daffy Duck first appeared in *Porky's Duck Hunt* (1937), but only later became the crafty sociopath that we know and love. As with the characters, it is not possible here to do justice to all the people who made Warner cartoons so memorable. Instead, I've chosen to focus on Tex Avery and Chuck Jones, because of their personal standing in the animation field. In no way should this be seen as a slight to the talents of directors such as Isadore 'Friz' Freleng, Bob Clampett (who later created the sublimely silly *Beany and Cecil*), Robert McKimson and Frank Tashlin (the only animator at Warners who went on to become a live-action director, notably of several Jerry Lewis films). Other important contributors include gag-writers such as Mike Maltese and Tedd Pierce, layout artists like Maurice Noble and Hawley Pratt, animators such as Ben Washam and Abe Levitow, incredible turn-on-a-dime musical scores by Carl Stalling and, of course, the 'vocal characterizations' of Mel Blanc.

Tex Avery

Frederick Bean Avery was born in Texas on 26 February 1908. Just as Orson Welles famously compared being a movie director to having 'the biggest toy train set a boy ever had', Avery treated animation as if the universe itself was at his command and all laws of physics, reality and movie grammar were his to bend and break as he saw fit. Characters would run so fast that they would skid off the film into the soundtrack sprockets, run out of Technicolor into black and white, even stop in mid-action to clobber a member of the audience who insisted on getting out of his seat. As Disney had leant depth to their animation with the use of the multiplane camera, Avery's influence at Warners and MGM saw animators tackling depth by creating scenes of such frenzied action that it threatened to spill out of the flat screen and into the real world.

Much play has been made that Avery never created a long-running animated character and that the one character that he did create (Screwy Squirrel) he disliked so much that he actually killed him off onscreen. But Avery did create characters: Droopy the depressive dog (Poodle? Bloodhound? In *The Chump Champ* he's one, In *North-West Hounded Police* he's the other). He also produced more iconic creations such as the eyeball-ejaculating Wolf forever banging his head against the table in a frenzy of sexual excitement, and the object of his affections, be she *Swing-Shift Cinderella* or *Red-Hot Riding Hood*, the curvaceous babe with a hard edge. As Jessica Rabbit (a tribute to Avery's style) in *Who Framed Roger Rabbit?* says: 'I'm not bad, I'm just drawn that way'.

Avery began as an unsuccessful cartoonist, unable to draw interest from newspapers in several cities. Hearing that the dubious Charles Mintz was hiring, he got a temporary ink-and-painting job. From there he moved to the Walter Lantz Studio, becoming an in-betweener and backgrounder on Oswald the Lucky Rabbit shorts. Through good fortune, he had a rapid rise at Lantz. Through equally good fortune, the Lantz Studio didn't mind what Avery did, so long as the shorts brought in revenue. Consequently, Avery was allowed to tear up the rule-book and do whatever he felt like. Despite his gift to astonish and amuse, Avery was a deeply insecure person. At Warners, he would habitually carry papers around with him so he would look like he was working, so great was his fear of being sacked. This was despite the fact that no one was more highly valued at the studio.

Avery moved to Warners in 1935, after Lantz refused him a pay-rise. He persuaded Leon Schlesinger to hire him as an animation director. Here he worked alongside

Friz Freleng and Hal King. Avery's team was assigned a termite-ridden bungalow, which became immortalised as 'Termite Terrace'. Warners couldn't compete with Disney on their home-turf (story and character), so Avery and his team flooded their films with rapid-fire gags and surrealism, ensuring that Warners would find their own audience.

Avery's first cartoon for Warners was *Gold Diggers of '49* (1936), a vehicle for the slightly dull characters Porky and Beans (a hilariously named pig and cat respectively). Both had featured in previous cartoons and Warners had hopes of continuing their careers. Avery soon changed that. For *Gold Diggers*, he aged them from infants to grown-up characters and used more sophisticated humour. His thinking was that Disney had cornered the market for small kids so Warners had to aim for the big kids; this idea soon spread through Warners' animation studio. Beans was soon retired, but Porky Pig became a star in his own right in shorts such as Bob Clampett's *Porky in Wackyland* (1938) and an able foil to the zaniness of Daffy Duck from *Porky's Duck Hunt* onwards. Mel Blanc later replaced the genuinely-stammering Joe Dougherty to give Porky his trademark 'Th-th-th-that's all folks' catchphrase.

It was over Warners' biggest star that Avery quit the studio. He had ended *The Heckling Hare* (1941) with the appearance that Bugs Bunny was plummeting to his death. In one of his rare moments of intervention, Schlesinger, concerned at what audiences might think, cut the ending. Enraged by this interference, Avery walked out.

He was immediately hired by MGM – a far dimmer light in the animation firmament and presided over by the famously humourless Fred Quimby. He didn't 'get' *Tom and Jerry* and found Avery's humour completely beyond the pale. But despite this, and the restrictions imposed on the film industry as a whole by the Hays Office, Avery somehow managed to produce some of the most subversive and racy cartoons within a studio system. Aided by gag-writers such as Heck Allen and Rich Hogan and animators like Preston Blair and Walter Clinton, it was at MGM that Avery's obsession with speed in cartoons reached its demented peak. He is quoted as having calculated that the shortest reaction time for an audience to actually take something in is five frames of film. A fine example of this reaction time put into practice is *Bad Luck Blackie* (1949), probably the pinnacle of slapstick animation.

The plot, in short, tells of a small white kitten who is persecuted by a sadistic bulldog (whose wheezing laugh was voiced by Avery). After various indignities, the kitten meets Bad Luck Blackie, a black cat who guarantees that as soon as he crosses the bulldog's path, bad luck will befall him. And befall him it does, each time Blackie is summoned and crosses his path, another object falls from the sky and clobbers the dog. When the dog paints Blackie white and prepares to mangle him, the kitten paints himself black and the punishment continues.

The dog's reaction time is about the same as the audience's. The cat crosses his path and he pauses, glances up, gasps with horror . . . and then smack. The object is always just out of frame to begin with, but by the end of nearly the fifth frame, he has been clobbered again. We get just enough warning to anticipate what the next object will be before it hits. The gag, of course, is that each object must top the last, in size, unlikeliness and damage that it perpetrates on the dog. We naturally graduate from a flowerpot at the start to a battleship at the end. This comic escalation was just part of Avery's repertoire but he always returned to it, particularly in matters of speed (the increasing rapidity of Wolfie's attempt to escape Droopy in *Dumb-Hounded*, the mouse's appearances in *Slap-Happy Lion*, etc.), until the humour comes simply from the frenetic blur of activity onscreen.

Avery's influence soon started to rub off on the animators working on MGM's Tom and Jerry shorts for Hanna and Barbera. Ironically, while that series won seven Oscars for animated film, Avery only won one, for *Blitz Wolf* (1942). He also ran into censorship troubles with *Red Hot Riding Hood* (1943), as Wolfie's reaction to Red's nightclub act (her performance was rotoscoped from a genuine dance routine) was deemed too phallic. This was despite several other similar previous Wolfie performances and the fact that several of these cartoons were being made with the view to entertaining troops overseas.

Increasingly stressed by working for Quimby, Avery took a year off in 1950 but returned to find his livelihood under threat from TV. Increasingly unhappy, he moved back to Walter Lantz for a short time after MGM closed in 1954. From there he joined Cascade, who produced animated commercials. Despite winning an award for a Raid insecticide commercial, he had begun to drink heavily. In 1977, he joined Hanna-Barbera as a gag-writer and it was William Hanna who found him collapsed at the office in 1980. He was subsequently diagnosed with terminal lung cancer and died in hospital on 26 August 1980.

Chuck Jones

One of the most recognizable names in animation, was born Charles Martin Jones in Spokane, Washington on 21 September 1912. He was one of the few animators of the period to have received formal art training. Aged 15, he had attended classes at the Chouinard Art Institute, Los Angeles. Importantly, he was taught about anatomy and how to represent it. His family also lived near the Charles Chaplin studio, which gave the young Jones many opportunities to watch comedies being filmed and to gain lessons in comedic timing. Like Tex Avery, Jones would become obsessive about timing visual gags to the exact frame.

After graduating, Jones was unemployed until a friend (Fred Kopietz, later a Disney employee) told him that he could get a job drawing for a living by working for an animation studio.

In 1931, he was hired by Celebrity Pictures. Its owner was the financially slippery Pat Powers but the animation studio was run by Ub Iwerks. Also working there was Grim Natwick, the legendary creator of *Betty Boop*. Jones started as a cel washer (as celluloid was costly, it was common for animation companies to recycle them), but Natwick, himself formally trained, recognised Jones' talents and soon he was promoted to an in-betweener. Natwick also showed Jones how to animate his understanding of movement.

Unfortunately, Jones was soon fired. For a while, he worked as a portraitist. Then his defining moment arrived when, in 1933, he landed a job at Leon Schlesinger Productions. With Harman and Ising having just left, Friz Freleng had been made animation director for both *Loony Tunes* and *Merrie Melodies*. To ease the pressure on him, he brought in some colleagues from his days at the Kansas City Film Ad Company: Ben 'Bugs' Hardaway and Tubby Millar. He also roped in staff at Schlesinger's, including Tex Avery, Bob Clampett, Robert McKimson and, as in-betweener, Chuck Jones. (The supposed origin of Bugs Bunny's name comes from a Hardaway sketch for use by animator Charles Thorson. To identify it, Thorson wrote on the bottom of the sketch 'Bugs's Bunny'.) Termite Terrace was the least Schlesinger-infested part of the company. He had little interest in Avery's team's output beyond their success with audiences. Avery's experimental approach to animation proved a perfect influence for Jones' own burgeoning style.

Jones' responsibilities increased until, in 1936, he directed his first animated film, *The Night Watchman*. It was a slight effort, but not without charm, telling of a kitten bullied by mice until he is pushed too far. Part of its running time was padded out with a lamentable song-and-dance routine that showed Jones was still uncertain about how far he could break with convention.

During the Second World War, like many animators, Jones was involved in propaganda cartoons which were issued as part of Warners compilations for troops overseas. The Private Snafu cartoons, many of them written by Dr Seuss (Theodore Geisel), involved the incompetent private demonstrating how not to do a variety of things. Jones directed 12 of the 26 episodes produced, and it was during this time that he formed a friendship with Geisel which would lead to greater things years later.

As well as working on films for Bugs and Elmer (such as *Elmer's Candid Camera* (1940)) and Daffy and Porky (*My Favourite Duck* (1942)), Jones had also introduced some new characters. The first, an underwhelming mouse called Sniffles, debuted in *Naughty But Mice* (1939) and lasted until 1946. After the war, other characters that Jones introduced were more popular including the power-hungry Marvin Martian, usually pitted against Bugs – as in *Haredevil Hare* (1948) or the equally power-hungry Daffy Duck (see *Duck Dodgers in the 24th½ Century, 1953*). More popular still was the love-hungry skunk Pepe Le Pew. Usually pitted against a female cat who just happened to have had a white stripe of paint splashed down her back, he first appeared in *Odor-able Kitty* (1945). Jones also took Daffy Duck's problems with Bugs Bunny to a whole new level in *Duck Amuck* (1953). One of Jones' finest, Daffy plays the 'star' of a cartoon whose animator continually alters the setting, the story and Daffy as he sees fit. After endless punishments and misunderstandings are meted out to Daffy he pleads for the faceless animator to reveal himself. We pull back to the studio to reveal Bugs. 'Ain't I a stinker?' he laughs. As far as exploring the sadistic relationship between animator and creation, *Duck Amuck* stood alone until Daniel Greaves' *Manipulation* (1992); but it's still the funniest.

Jones' greatest contribution to the hall of animated characters are the Road Runner & Coyote cartoons. More specifically, the obsessive-compulsive character of Wile E Coyote, created with one of Schlesinger's finest gag-writers, Mike Maltese. They were famously compared to the works of Samuel Beckett by one critic. While the Coyote had appeared opposite Bugs Bunny and alongside Sam the Sheepdog (as 'Ralph Wolf'), his real home was the vast, desolate stretches of the stylised American West depicted in the Road Runner cartoons. Here, it is not Road Runner who matters but Coyote's obsession and its painful consequences. The continual search for the unobtainable, the continual ordering of faulty Acme gadgets to aid his obsession, the continual failure and physical punishment that he suffers as a result – an unending, perfectly enclosed circle of Hell. From *Fast and Furry-ous* (1949) to *Chariots of Fur* (1994), the Coyote never learned, never stopped obsessing.

It was also here that Jones' obsession with timing was perfected. The Coyote cartoons always had at least one example of the perfect pause. Whether he was about to be flattened by a boulder or plummet off of another cliff, the Coyote would always, with impeccable timing, turn and look out of the screen, as if to draw us further into his situation, the second before disaster struck.

The Termite Terrace animators found unexpected benefits in the Coyote cartoons; they could be produced quite quickly. With Warners expecting each animation director to produce a cartoon every four weeks anything that took longer was seen as too expensive to make back its revenue. When a cartoon needed more time, the animators would rush out a Coyote cartoon in two weeks and keep the title on their worksheets so that they would have eight or so weeks spare to produce a cartoon requiring more attention. One such cartoon was *What's Opera Doc?* (1957), one of the finest of Jones' Bugs Bunny shorts. With great skill and craft, they manage to cram Wagner's Ring Cycle into seven minutes. Well, enough of it so Elmer as Siegfried can chase Bugs as Brunhilde, anyway.

As well as series characters, Jones occasionally produced one-offs that were equally popular. The prime example is *One Froggy Evening* (1955), a shaggy-frog story in which a construction worker finds an all-singing, all-dancing frog bricked up in the foundation of a building he is helping to demolish. Thinking that he has found his fortune, the man tries various ways to catapult the frog (and himself) to stardom, with agents, audiences, etc., but each time the frog refuses to perform. It just sits there and croaks. Only when it is alone with the man does it launch into its song-and-dance routine. Finally, homeless, broke and half-mad, the man bricks the frog up once more. Years later, a man helping to lay new foundations for a building uncovers a frog in the brickwork. It launches into a song-and-dance routine . . .

Outside of the Roadrunner-Coyote cartoons, *One Froggy Evening* is the main cartoon where Jones comments continually on the sheer cussedness of life and of mankind's continuing optimism in the face of all evidence to the contrary. The laughter derived from the cartoon comes more from recognition and pity than from the frog's antics.

Another one-off that Jones produced during the period was the near-abstract *High Note* (1960), which tells of a drunken high note whose erratic behaviour scuppers a performance of Strauss' *Blue Danube*. In 1965, he would win an Oscar for a similar cartoon, *The Dot and the Line*, which he made for MGM.

In 1953, Jack Warner closed down the studio, convinced that audiences no longer required animation now that 3-D had arrived. It took him four months to realise his mistake and re-open the studio. The studio was finally closed in 1962. Chuck Jones set up Tower 12 Productions with Les Goldman, mainly to produce shorts for MGM (who had shut down their own animation studio in 1954). It was during this period that Jones made the off-key *Tom and Jerry* shorts.

1962 also saw the start of Chuck Jones Enterprises which, like Hanna-Barbera, was dedicated to producing animation for TV. A sub-division, Chuck Jones Productions did produce cartoons for the cinema as well as animated sequences for live-action features – including *Mrs Doubtfire* (1993). CJE has produced some memorable TV animation, including adaptations of popular children's books such as Norton Juster's *The Phantom Tollbooth* (1969) (with Abe Levitow) which did justice both to Juster's writing and Jules Feiffer's illustrations.

Probably the most memorable TV special that Jones produced during this period was with Dr Seuss. *How The Grinch Stole Christmas!* (1966), like *The Snowman*, regularly appears every Christmas on TV. It is a faultless adaptation, with the characters immediately recognisable as Seuss' originals but with just enough of Jones' in them to make them recognisably his as well. Seuss' joyous poetry being read by Boris Karloff is an added touch of inspiration.

Jones continued producing animation into the 1990s, including further outings for Bugs Bunny and Daffy Duck (who makes several interruptions during the end credits for Joe Dante's *Gremlins 2 – The New Batch* (1990), the original of which featured a cameo by Jones). There have also been compilations of his best work, the finest being *The Bugs Bunny/Road Runner Movie* (1979), which features *Duck Amuck, Duck Dodgers in the 24ᵗʰ1/2 Century* and *What's Opera Doc?* He lived long enough to see the work that he and others produced at Warners become valued beyond the ephemera they believed they were making at the time. Jones died in 2002.

Hanna and Barbera

William Hanna and Joseph Barbera's names have been inextricably linked since 1940 when they made their first cartoon together: *Puss Gets the Boot*. It featured a mouse called Jerry and a cat called, er . . . Jasper. Their paths to MGM had been circuitous, but once together their rise was assured and they would come to rule the field of TV animation almost without competition.

Hanna was born on 14 July 1910 in New Mexico. His family moved to Los Angeles in 1919 and, while working with his father in construction in 1929, Hanna heard about a new animation studio. The company, Harman-Ising was contracted to produce animated shorts for Warner Brothers. Despite a lack of art training, Hanna got in on the bottom rung. Soon he was promoted to head of the ink-and-paint department. His way with gags made him one of Harman-Ising's storymen also.

In 1933, Harman-Ising pulled out of Schlesinger's contract in a row over budgets. Although Schlesinger offered Hanna a job in his new animation team, Hanna stuck with Harman-Ising. In 1934, the company landed a contract with MGM to produce the *Happy Harmonies* series. One of these, *To Spring* (released June 1936) was Hanna's first short as director. Hanna had no such loyalty when Harman-Ising were dropped by MGM in 1937. He moved to MGM's new animation studio as a director of animation.

Joseph Barbera took a different route. Born in Little Italy, New York on 24 March 1911, Barbera had a natural talent for drawing but looked set for a career in finance. He attended art classes after work and spent his lunch hours pitching cartoons to various New York magazines. After making a sale to the influential *Collier's* magazine, editors' doors were open to him. Barbera left his job and became a freelance sketch artist.

However, the better pay and job security of the animation industry attracted him. His drawing style – quick, spare and fluid – meant that he was perfectly suited to animation's requirements. After an extremely brief stint with the Fleischer studio (four days) and a swift rise through the ranks at the down-at-heel Van Beuren studio, Barbera found himself unemployed once more when Van Beuren closed in 1936. He was about to try for Disney in California when Paul Terry hired him for Terrytoons. What neither of them foresaw was the rapaciousness of MGM's new animation studio, run by MGM executive Fred Quimby. Having already hired most of the old Harman-Ising staff, Quimby got a friend of his at

Terrytoons to lure away their best animators too, Barbera amongst them.

What happened after Quimby had assembled this team was a series of failures that almost destroyed the studio before it had even found its stride. Quimby, it is rumoured, had little time for cartoons anyway (he really wanted to make boxing pictures) and assumed that animating a popular comic strip would be an immediate success. He was wrong. Technically, MGM's adaptations of Rudolph Dirks' *The Katzenjammer Kids* was fine, but the project was out-of-step with what the public wanted and the series flopped badly. Quimby tried a couple of other cartoon strips with no success and was soon begging Harman and Ising to come back to work.

What the public really wanted was funny animals. Hanna and Barbera had become friends during their time at MGM, and together they threw out some ideas for their own cartoon. The aforementioned *Puss Gets the Boot* was well received and, with a name change for the cat, *Tom and Jerry* came into being. Here was what Quimby had been grasping for but not seeing: cartoon characters with *character*. A plucky, quick-witted mouse and a long-suffering, short-tempered cat, both of whom drew audience sympathies. They may have wanted Jerry to win, but related to Tom because he has noticeably human foibles. Tom and Jerry are Hanna-Barbera's finest hour. The shorts, made between 1940 and 1952, are mainly fast-paced, beautifully timed and staggeringly violent pieces of slapstick (my nomination for the most brutal, and therefore funniest, is *Cue Ball Cat*, but feel free to argue amongst yourselves). Thirteen of the shorts were nominated for Oscars and seven won (*Yankee Doodle Mouse* (1943), *Mouse Trouble* (1944), *Quiet Please* (1945), *Cat Concerto* (1946), *The Little Orphan* (1948), *The Two Mouseketeers* (1951) and *Johann Mouse* (1952)). The two adversaries were also popular enough to have cameos in MGM live-action films; Jerry dancing with Gene Kelly in *Anchors Aweigh* (1945); both of them with Kelly in *Invitation to the Dance* (1953) and swimming with Esther Williams in *Dangerous When Wet* (1953).

Tom and Jerry would be revived in 1962 in a series of off-key shorts directed by Chuck Jones. In the 1990s they were reunited for *The Tom and Jerry Movie*, a grotesque aberration where the two characters actually spoke, sang and teamed up to help a small orphan girl. As I said in the introduction: Small things. Hitting each other. Apparently this is a hard concept to grasp – at least to the geniuses who came up with this monstrosity. To add insult to injury, the pair were recently seen advertising Ford cars. Whether this is as bad or worse than seeing the Looney Tunes characters whoring themselves for Warner Village cinemas I shall leave to you to decide.

By the mid-50s television had begun to eat into cinema's profits. Although MGM's studio was one of the most successful, it was shut down in 1957. Hanna and Barbera could have had their pick of other studios (minus Tom and Jerry, who were owned by MGM), but instead they headed towards TV. They set up Hanna–Barbera with the sole aim of producing animation for television.

Their first series, *The Ruff and Reddy Show*, was for NBC and was mainly a repackaging of old Columbia cinema shorts, with a five-minute episode of *Ruff* (a dog) *and Reddy* (a cat), a comedy crime-fighting team. From the outset, Hanna-Barbera shot in colour (one of their few extravagances) in order to capitalise on repeat showings and the associated royalties.

And from this point onwards their output was held together by their knack of creating popular cartoon characters and a neat line in catchphrases and one-liners. If corners could be cut in the animation process, then they would be cut. Scenes (and scenery) would be recycled in order to keep animation costs to a minimum. Anyone who has watched a chase scene in, for example, *Scooby-Doo, Where are You!* (sic) where the characters race down an endless hallway with a grandfather clock every five yards will know what I mean. The fact that the gang have stumbled into an architectural anomaly as eerie as anything in Mark Z Danielewski's *House of Leaves* seems to pass unnoticed as they're too busy being chased by Mr Dithers the caretaker with a sheet over his head.

The real dip in quality in TV cartoons had started once the three big US networks had started running back-to-back cartoons on Saturday mornings, around the mid-60s. Demand far outstripped production and, with most of the classic animators getting older, people were hired to write and animate who had no background in the tradition. Despite their shortcomings (and that includes Scrappy-Doo), Hanna-Barbera were, until *The Simpsons* aired, the undisputed kings of the animated TV featurette. The titles alone of many of the shows are enough to send a warm glow of nostalgia over many a thirtysomething: *The Huckleberry Hound Show*, *The Flintstones*, *Top Cat* (aka: *Boss Cat* in the UK to avoid confusion with a brand of cat food), *The Yogi Bear Show*, *The Jetsons*, *Dastardly and Muttley* and Their Flying Machines (aka: Stop the Pigeon), Wacky Races, The Addams Family, Wait 'til Your Father Gets Home (H-B's most adult-oriented series), Hong Kong Phooey . . . Following their lead, other companies later tried to keep up (or down, as their animation looked even cheaper), such as Filmation (from 1962) which made He-Man and the Masters of the Universe and Ruby-Spears which brought you the werewolf Scooby Fangface (1977).

The studio has also branched out into feature-length animation, dipping their toes into the water with their brain-meltingly awful adaptation of Alice in Wonderland, Or What's a Nice Girl Like You Doing in a Place Like This (1966) and the slightly better Charlotte's Web (1973). More recent outings have included Scooby-Doo and the Ghoul School (1988) and Johnny Quest versus the Cyber Insects (1995). However, the animation remains painfully simplistic and the plots can barely stagger through their 80 plus minutes of air-time. There have also been occasional forays into live-action versions of their more popular series, such as the appalling Flintstones movies. Unfortunately, each new attempt to reinject life into the old formulas is effectively scuppered whenever a 'Golden Age' Tom and Jerry cartoon is screened and, for seven minutes, beautifully animated chaos reigns. That's when you realise that no amount of snappy one-liners and catchphrases can better what Hanna and Barbera had at MGM.

William Hanna died in North Hollywood on 22 March 2001.

UPA

Following the end of the Second World War, a new war that had been brewing for some time came to a head. In 1946, mass production of televisions began in earnest and their sales increased accordingly. Cinema attendance began to drop. The Hollywood studio system monopoly on audiences, previously able to control every aspect of production, exhibition and distribution, was effectively broken up. The Supreme Court ruled against them in *United States* v. *Paramount et al*, in 1948. Animated shorts were one of the first casualties of this ruling; their role as fillers on cinema programmes dried up as costs rose. Animation studios were drastically reduced and often closed altogether. Disney began to focus on animated features and branched out into live-action films for children. The studio's first two experiments in this area, *Song of the South* (1946) and *So Dear to My Heart* (1949), used animated sections within a live-action framing device as if to test the water with audiences. This lead to *Treasure Island* (1950). The same period saw Disney expand into amusement parks with Disneyland opening in Anaheim, California in 1955, and nature documentaries. (One of which is rumoured to have started the whole 'lemming jumping off cliffs' myth.)

The late 40s and early 50s also saw other changes afoot in animation. Most notable was the success of UPA (United Productions of America). This company was formed in 1944 by Dave Hilberman, Zachary Schwartz and Stephen Bosustow. Former Disney employees, they had left during the 1941 strike and joined forces to produce an animated short for Franklin Delano Roosevelt's election campaign: *Hell Bent for Election*. Their early work was mainly educational and propaganda shorts but traces could already be seen of the new direction that they were taking. This direction was influenced by much of the changes in modern culture around them. The 50s saw the rise of more cerebral comedians such as Lenny Bruce and Mort Sahl. Cartoonists were developing styles outside the traditional rounded forms and the works of Saul Steinberg and Jules Feiffer also heralded a shift in the style of animated characters.

UPA's newly hired staff included artists such as John Hubley (who, with his wife Faith, would go on to make more avant-garde and philosophical films such as *Eggs* (1971) and *Everybody Rides the Carousel* (1976)), Jules Engel (whose interest in abstract art would lead him eventually to make pure abstract films such as *Landscape* (1971) using pulsing colours on blotting paper), Bill Hurtz (who would bring James Thurber's drawings to life in *A Unicorn in the Garden* (1953)) and Paul Julien, who would work on UPA's impressive adaptation of Poe's *The Tell-Tale Heart* (1953). Directed by Ted Parmalee and narrated by James Mason, it used limited animation and expressionistic sets to great effect.

In 1946, Hilberman and Schwartz left and Bosustow remained as executive producer. His skills as a scriptwriter had been proven at Walter Lantz and, from 1934, at Disney, where he had worked on several features, including *Snow White* and *Fantasia*. At UPA, he was a strong believer in allowing his filmmakers to express themselves. He did away with the assembly-line animation method and encouraged teams to form themselves according to their films' requirements.

In 1948, UPA's fortunes improved when Columbia agreed to distribute their films. In their cartoons of this time such as *Robin Hoodlum* (1948) their artwork was already very stylised and the comedy more cerebral than slapstick. In 1949, their most popular character made his debut in *Ragtime Bear*. Mr Magoo, the baldheaded, short-sighted grouch, gravel-voiced by character actor Jim Backus, was far-removed from the glamorous characters at studios like Disney. It was almost as if Elmer Fudd had been made the hero. His popular success led to a ten-year career, during which time UPA's star ascended and descended once more.

The success of its stylised approach came in 1951–2 with two short films *Gerald McBoing Boing* (directed by Bobe Cannon, who would also direct UPA's adaptation of Ludwig Bemelman's *Madeline*, 1952) and John Hubley's *Rooty Toot Toot*. *Gerald* featured a child who, unable to speak, uttered various sound-effects noises such as 'boing boing', much to the distraction of his parents. It was based upon a story by Dr Seuss. *Rooty* was a version of the ballad *Frankie and Johnnie*. In both, strongly anti-realist backgrounds such as large blocks of colour, were combined with limited animation to demonstrate the modernist approach of the directors.

By the mid-50s UPA had lost many of its best artists, including Hubley (blacklisted by HUAC) and was reduced to repetitions of Mister Magoo (1956–58), in a TV series based on *Gerald McBoing Boing*, and advertising. In 1958, they closed their New York and London offices. A feature film based around Mister Magoo: *1001 Arabian Nights* (1959) bombed at the box office. Bosustow retired in 1961 to produce educational films. UPA continued in a much diminished form, producing far less distinctive TV series. Their influential style during their peak period, while not always finding favour with audiences (especially those who preferred traditional animation), certainly found enough imitators. Even Disney aped it in their Oscar-winning *Toot, Whistle, Plunk and Boom* (1954).

Britain and Canada

*'Animation is not the art of drawings that move, but rather
the art of movements that are drawn.'*

Norman McLaren

In the early 1900s British animation had been mostly for
internal distribution. Most notable among these animators
was George Ernest Studdy, whose animated dog, Bonzo,
was both fluidly animated and displayed its creator's
knowledge of cinematic language. By the '30s most British
animation was being produced for advertising. Those
breaking away from this included Anson Dyer, whose
character, Sam Small, was an accident-prone soldier,
voiced by Stanley Holloway. A lack of native artists was
made up for in Britain becoming a stopover for foreign
artists such as Lotte Reiniger, Anthony Gross and John
Halas. Born in Budapest, Halas moved to Britain just
before the outbreak of World War II. In 1940, he
founded Halas & Batchelor with British animator and
scriptwriter Joy Batchelor. They produced many well-
regarded propaganda and information shorts but it is
for their feature-length adaptation of George Orwell's
anti-Stalinist satire *Animal Farm* (1954) that their studio
is best remembered (see *Animator's Dozen*). Another

immigrant was New Zealander Len Lye. Lye's work for the GPO Film Unit, such as *A Colour Box* and *Rainbow Dance* (1936), whilst being adverts for GPO services were triumphs of abstract animation and paved the way for work by Norman McLaren. McLaren's later move to Canada would result in the National Film Board of Canada becoming the launch pad for many successful animators. As such, the rise of both countries' animated work is inextricably linked. In this chapter, therefore, there are representatives of both countries' animation, as well as some examples of those who 'passed through'.

Norman McLaren

One of the great innovators of animation, McLaren began his career working for John Grierson at the GPO (General Post Office) film unit, as did Len Lye. During his career he amassed 147 awards for his work, a record that remains unbroken. He was born in Stirling in 1914. Enrolling at the Glasgow School of Art in 1933 he discovered a discarded 16mm movie projector. Possessing no camera, he acquired some old film stock and soaked off the emulsion. Thus prepared, he painted directly onto the film. While this first work in animation did not result in anything worth screening, he realised that the technique had enough potential to pursue. During his course he made several short live-action experimental films and won a prize at the Second Glasgow Amateur Film Festival in 1935. At the next year's festival he came to the attention of one of the judges, acclaimed documentary maker John Grierson. Grierson had been made head of the GPO film unit. McLaren submitted two shorts for exhibition at the festival, *Camera Making Whoopee* (a special-effects-laden showpiece) and *Colour Cocktail* (an abstract combination of live action and coloured dots synched to a gramophone record). Grierson lambasted *Whoopee* but selected *Cocktail* as the event's winner. He also offered McLaren a job at the film unit. Work for the GPO consisted of films that would advertise various services that the GPO offered to the public (such as Len Lye's *Rainbow Dance*, which advertised the Post Office Savings Bank). McLaren started work in 1936. His first work for Grierson involved going to Spain as a cameraman for Ivor Montagu. His footage of the Spanish Civil War formed the pro-Republican documentary *Defence of Madrid* (1937). The bloodshed he witnessed there also deepened his pacifist stance – a side of him which can be clearly seen in anti-war films such as *Hell unLtd* (1936) and the Oscar-winning *Neighbours* (1952).

McLaren's first professional animated work was *Love on the Wing* (1938), again using artwork drawn directly onto the film stock and was intended to encourage people to send telegrams. By this point, Grierson had been appointed the first Commissioner of the National Film Board of Canada (NFBC) and was replaced at the GPO by Alberto Cavalcanti. He thus missed the furore that McLaren's film created, as it contained the image of a pair of scissors metamorphosing (very briefly) into male genitalia. The Postmaster General suppressed the film but it is now regarded as a classic of innovation. *Love on the Wing* was also the first of McLaren's films to explore 'animated sound', by which he added his own sound coding to the edge of the film stock. He would develop this idea further for later shorts including *Blinkety Blank* (1952) and *Synchromy* (1971).

With the Second World War looming, McLaren made one last short for the GPO; *Mony a Pickle* (1938), before moving to New York. Once there, he contacted Grierson to see if there was any work at the NFBC, but there were no vacancies. He was commissioned by the Museum of Non-Objective Painting (later to become the Guggen-heim Museum) to produce several experimental shorts. These were all about two minutes long and also explored his technique of animated sound. McLaren admitted that it was also an economy measure as 'I had no money for the sound-tape'. Worse, the grants for works such as *Allegro* (1939) and *Dots* (1940) weren't enough to keep him solvent. McLaren was forced to take on 'in-betweening' work at commercial animation studios to help finance his own films.

By 1941, the situation at the NFBC had altered. The Canadian Government desperately needed money for the war effort and turned to NFBC to produce propaganda films encouraging the public to buy war bonds. Grierson felt that McLaren's lightness of touch might soften up the audience to other subject matter in the packages of movies that the NFBC showed at works canteens and other meeting places. While McLaren was initially resistant to creating pro-war propaganda, he relented and, from 1941, he would work for the NFBC until his retirement.

Of the works he created until 1945, some were open propaganda *V for Victory* (1941), *Keep Your Mouth Shut* (1944) and others less so, for example *Hen Hop* (1942). In 1943, he helped birth the NFBC's animation unit and

directed two of a series of animations based around traditional French folk songs: *C'est L'aviron* (*This is the Oar*) and
Alouette (*The Lark*) (both 1944).

While Grierson left the NFBC at the end of the war,
McLaren remained. Over the next 30 years he would direct
over 40 animated shorts and help make the NFBC a
breeding ground for new animators. Among those who
benefited from his patronage were George Dunning,
Caroline Leaf and Frédéric Back. In his own work, he
continued to be a great innovator. For *Blinkety Blank* he
reversed his technique of drawing onto blank film by
scratching onto the black celluloid. The images, mostly one
frame in length, were spaced out through the film to create
small visual explosions in which the viewer through persistence of vision sometimes discerns movement. His restless
experimentalism led to a series of austere abstract animations made with his regular collaborator Evelyn Lambart.
Lines Vertical (1960) came from the simplest of ideas – a
single vertical line moving slowly then rapidly. It eventually
expands to choreograph a whole group of vertical lines.
This led to *Lines Horizontal* (1962) – the lines rerouted
through a prism but giving the film a very different 'mood'.
A third film, *Mosaic* (1965), combined vertical and horizontal lines but focused on their intersections.

Arguably McLaren's two finest films are at a polar
opposite to these coolly formal experiments. Exploring
and reinventing human movement, they remain fresh and
fascinating to this day. *Pas de Deux* (1965) and *Neighbours*
(1952) differ wildly in their approaches.

For *Pas de Deux* the innovation for once took place in
the film laboratory after the film had been made. Two

ballet dancers were filmed going through basic ballet movements, side-lit to cast them almost in silhouette. The frames were then printed in multiple superimposition (up to ten frames at a time). Thus the echoes of the dancers' movements become complex geometric shapes, the choreography tangible.

For *Neighbours*, McLaren pixilated two actors. Although pixilation is often used for the filming of all 3-D objects, it is normally applied to the act of animating actors. The process usually involves filming actors in such a way that their movements appear jerky. For *Neighbours* McLaren gained added effectiveness by filming his actors jumping in the air and cutting out the moments where they touched the ground, thus giving the appearance they were floating through the air. *Neighbours* tells of two neighbours who discover a flower growing between their two properties. Their joy at discovering this thing of beauty degenerates into a battle over ownership of the flower. From fencing off their properties so that the flower is enclosed on their side (McLaren also pixilated the fences, literally being 'drawn' by the neighbours), they start to attack each other as each seeks to defend 'their' flower. From there, it is a small step to attacking and killing each others families and then a vicious brawl (during which war paint sprouts on their faces with increasingly characterised aggressiveness) which both kills them and crushes the flower. As they lay dead, the ground rises up and buries them, the fence posts become their grave markers and flowers grow on both their graves. McLaren's message to 'Love Your Neighbour' is animated in many different languages.

McLaren made his last film, *Narcissus*, in 1983. It ran at 22 minutes and used ballet dancers as well as many of the techniques that he had developed during his career to tell the legend of the youth who loves only himself. Although the tale was far removed from McLaren's own personality, the film itself acted as a recap on his career as one of animation's most versatile creators. He died in Montreal in 1987. In his lifetime he had frequently challenged the accepted idea of animation to produce thoughtful and outstanding works of art. In 1973 he was made a Companion of the Order of Canada and his influence upon a generation of animators extended well beyond the NFBC.

Caroline Leaf

One of the most individual animators to emerge from Norman McLaren's tutelage at the National Film Board of Canada, Caroline Leaf made her first film while a student at Harvard in 1968. Titled *Sand or Peter and the Wolf*, it was created using sand manipulated over a lightbox. Thus lit from below, she was able to tell the story in near-silhouette. In 1972, she moved to Montreal at the invitation of the National Film Board of Canada, for whom she worked until 1991.

Many of her later films have refined her sand technique, perhaps the strongest of these being *The Owl Who Married a Goose* (*Le Mariage du Hibou*, 1974) which was based on an Inuit legend. The goose produces a perfectly healthy brood of goslings and the owl, not adapted for either long-distance flight or water, struggles to keep up and eventually drowns. The dialogue, in Inuit, renders some scenes rather oblique but Leaf's animation of the characters and shifts in setting are confidently realised. While Leaf's animation played up the tragic aspects of the story (the owl continually asserting that all is well as he sinks to the bottom of the lake), the Inuit audiences reportedly find the story of the owl's inappropriate love very amusing.

Her next film, *The Street* (1976), won her a well-deserved Oscar. Adapted from a short story by Mordecai Richler, *The Street* tells of a Jewish family during a hot New York summer. Their daily lives revolve around the children's dying maternal grandmother who, although confined to bed, dominates their lives. The events are related from the memories of the youngest son who will inherit grandmother's room once she dies. The character is not as mercenary as this makes it sound and, once the grandmother finally dies, he is loath to move into the room because that's where she died. For this film, Leaf painted the watercolour artwork onto glass and filmed the results. If anything, the effect is even more impressive than with sand, filling *The Street* with movement and cinematic shifts of perspective (not least in a 'tracking shot' along the street itself as the boy comes home from school). It allows for the smallest observations of details, such as the imprints of the daughter's hands remaining on her pillow as she gets up, and for the dynamism of movement (such as the sheet flapping around the daughter as she pretends to be the grandmother's ghost). It also echoes the fluidity of memory (the child is Richler, recalling his childhood), as events flow from one another, with Leaf's animation acting as the conduit and thus making these transitions as seamless as possible (e.g. as the visiting nurse arrives and climbs the stairs, the dark space around her begins to form faces that move us on to the family's life downstairs). As with most of Leaf's tales, once the main event has taken place (here, the grandmother's death) the story ends. Her point has been made.

She returned to sand animation for *The Metamorphosis of Mr. Samsa* (1977), adapted from Kafka's short story. Like *The Owl . . .* it was told in greyscale, while its observation of realism owed more to *The Street*. Over the next few years, her animation work was balanced with several live-action films, including a documentary on the pianists, Kate and Anna McGarrigle, and contributing an animated section to *Interview* (1979), in which Leaf and filmmaker Veronica Soul interview each other about the loneliness of the creative process. Her next, and last to date, major work of animation was *Two Sisters* (*Entre Deux Soeurs*, 1990) utilised the McLaren-esque process of etching the images onto exposed film emulsion. It gave a dark, edgy aspect to what was a very dark and edgy drama about sibling rivalry. Since this time, Leaf has concentrated more on work for idents and advertising companies (including Benson & Hedges and Absolut Vodka); when time allows, she also produces sketches and oil-paintings. Given her ability to marshal such disparate materials into animation and to produce such startling results and that her influence can be felt in such varied NFBC animations as Gayle Thomas' etched *A Sufi Tale* (1980) and 'Co' Hoedeman's Oscar-winning *The Sandcastle* (*La Château De Sable*, 1977) it is to be hoped that we have not heard the last of her or her impressive experimental style.

George Dunning

Born in Toronto in 1920, Dunning should be forever remembered as the man who made *Yellow Submarine* (1968), one of the truly idiosyncratic animated features whose unique style has been pilfered ever since it was first released, most recently by *South Park*. He joined the National Film Board of Canada in 1942 and came under the tutelage of Norman McLaren. Here he made several short films, including some within the NFBC's continuing series of animations of popular French-Canadian folksongs – *Chants Populaires No. 2* (1942) and *Cadet Rouselle* (1946). He was also one of the few animators since Lotte Reiniger to work with silhouette animation with *Grim Pastures* (1944).

After a brief trip to Paris in 1948 where he met several European animators, including Paul Grimault, he founded Graphic Associates in Toronto with his former NFBC colleague Jim McKay. He later went to work on the UPA TV series *Gerald McBoing Boing* (based on the story by Dr Seuss). The original film, by Bobe Cannon, showed the influence of Post-Impressionist art and was far removed from the all-conquering Disney house style.

By 1955 when Dunning joined, UPA's star was in the descendent and they were relying on retreads of past glories. While many of their major artists had left, others who would later become famous were still working there. As well as Dunning, there was also Ernest Pintoff (who would direct the Mel Brooks' scripted/narrated short *The Critic*, (1963), Jimmy Teru Murakami (later to work for Roger Corman's New World company and to direct the impressive adaptation of Raymond Briggs' nuclear holocaust tale *When the Wind Blows*), Bill Melendez (who directed many of the better *Peanuts* animations, including the near-iconic *A Charlie Brown Christmas*) and Gene Deitch (who would work rewardingly with satirical cartoonist Jules Feiffer on *Munro,* 1960).

UPA sent Dunning to London in 1956 to open a UK office but when they changed owners the next year, Dunning had already started his own production company: TV Cartoons. It employed some old UPA staffers and did both programmes and adverts for television. Most of its acclaim came from the animated shorts it produced. Its first, the Dunning-directed *The Flying Man* (1962), was written by Stan Hayward, later to be forever remembered as the co-creator of the mighty *Henry's Cat* with Bob Godfrey. *The Flying Man* was rendered in watercolour on glass with no attempt to conceal how the artwork had arrived there.

Around 1964, ABC, along with King Features, began producing an animated TV series based on The Beatles. Each episode featured a couple of Beatles songs and the same 'zany' humour that had been a big part of the movies *A Hard Day's Night* and *Help!* with voices provided by Lance Percival amongst others. The Beatles' involvement in the series was minimal at best. And when Al Brodax of King Features became convinced that there was a feature film in the series, the Fab Four were hardly delighted with the idea. Although it was to be a co-production between King and Apple, The Beatles refused to have anything to do with it. George Martin, interviewed in 1995, stated that although Brian Epstein had committed them to the deal (as part of their contract with United Artists) and that they were expected to provide new songs, The Beatles said: 'Well, we're not going to write any decent songs, we're give them all the rejects that we didn't really want.'

Although their characters were voiced by actors, the Fab Four did finally agree to appear in a brief live sequence for the film's conclusion. They might have taken more notice had they realised that Dunning planned to take the film in a direction that the TV series had refused to go. He brought in Heinz Edelmann for design and his Pop Art/psychedelic sensibilities gave the film a look that, even today, remains the epitome of late 60s cool. In brief, the film tells of the Utopian Pepperland which is attacked by the evil Blue Meanies. To fetch help an emissary is dispatched in a yellow submarine. He finds the Beatles and much of the film is taken up with their voyage through strange lands, peopled by stranger creatures. After many tribulations, the Fab Four arrive in Pepperland and conquer the Blue Meanies with their musical stylings. *Yellow Submarine*'s beautifully realised other worlds and psychedelic sensibility can conquer even the most Beatles-resistant heart. The visual imaginings for the Beatles' songs played during the film (particularly *Lucy in the Sky with Diamonds* and *Eleanor Rigby*) and the surrealism in The Beatles' foes make it one of the few outstanding movies of the psychedelic era. It also opened up another road for animation to travel. Allegedly, even the Fab Four, when they finally deigned to see it, were chuffed with the result.

After the commercial success of *Yellow Submarine*, Dunning went on to create three well-received short films: *Moon Rock* (1971), *Damon the Mower* (1971) and *The*

Maggot (1972). *Damon the Mower* (based on a poem by Andrew Marvell) follows a similar artistic approach to *The Flying Man* – Damon scythes and landscapes explode on increasingly unstable sheets of numbered paper. *The Maggot* is a powerful tale of poverty and drug addiction. Here, Dunning's experimental nature gives us stark social commentary transfigured by the powerful elasticity into metaphor that animation easily allows but is rarely embraced by major studios.

His next venture was to be an adaptation of Shakespeare's *The Tempest*. But his death in 1979 robbed us of that achievement. He had animated a few brief minutes of footage. *The Tempest* would later form one of several adapted by other animators for BBC's *Animated Shakespeare* series.

Dunning's production company, TVC, would continue to make animated features, many of which would become 'traditional' favourites. Several had a particular bent towards the works of Raymond Briggs: *The Bear* (1998), *When the Wind Blows* (1986), *Father Christmas* (1991 – voiced by Mel Smith), and the seasonal TV favourite, *The Snowman* (1982). Of these, *When the Wind Blows* (directed by Jimmy T Murakami) is the most powerful. In a damning indictment of the *Protect and Survive* brochure issued by the British government in the event of a nuclear war, a working-class couple follow its instructions and die slowly of radiation poisoning and malnutrition. In the British tradition of films about nuclear holocausts and their after-effects, it stands comparison with *The War Game* and *Threads*.

TVC also made an adaptation of *The Wind in the Willows*

(1995) and its 'sequel' *The Willows in Winter* (1996) and an adaptation of Posey Simmons' entertaining story *Famous Fred* (1996), about a rock-'n'-roll-star cat.

Another company, Cosgrove-Hall, also made an adaptation of *Wind in the Willows*. It had charmingly designed stop-motion puppets. It later spawned a popular TV series, based more around Mr Toad (voiced by David Jason). Jason would also provide the voices for Cosgrove-Hall's most popular cel-animated series *Danger Mouse* (a spoof on James Bond and *The Avengers*) and *Count Duckula* (about a vegetarian vampire duck and his dozy retainers). Both were marked by witty scripts and appalling puns.

Despite the commercial success of *Yellow Submarine*, British animation didn't enjoy the boost that many had believed would follow; in fact it suffered a decline, with many animators being laid off from various studios. However, one animator, many of whose staff had worked on *Submarine*, did continue to enjoy success of a sort.

Paul Driessen

Born in Nijmegen on 30 March 1940, Driessen attended art school in Utrecht but came away with little that benefited his own burgeoning style. In the mid-60s he learnt animation techniques, and put them to good use, at the Hilversum-based advertising company, Cinecentrum. It was while he was working there that George Dunning saw some of his animation. Dunning invited him to London. Driessen arrived there the day before *Yellow Submarine* began preparation. He spent several months working on the production. During this time, Dunning's recollections of working for the National Film Board of Canada proved influential upon the young animator. He first returned to The Netherlands where, in 1970, he made his first independent feature, aided by a government grant. *The Story of Little John Bailey* (*Het Verhaal Van Kleine Yoghurt*) is about a child who starts a forest fire. When he later joined the National Film Board of Canada, his first films were equally ecologically minded: *The Missing Blue* (*Le Bleu Perdu*, 1972) and *Air!* (1972). But these films were atypical to his later work, when his style began to emerge. Driessen has said his style is so individual because he saw very few animated films when growing up. He did, however, encounter a good deal of Norman McLaren's work during his time with Dunning, which may go some way to explaining his playfulness and his continuing experimentation with what is possible to portray on screen. In *David* (1977) for instance, the protagonist is so small that the viewer is often left looking at a blank screen. David's presence is only announced by his hair, blowing in the wind, and his constant commentary.

What sets Driessen's work apart is the constant flow of ideas and the jittery nature of his animation which gives his characters a sense of nervous motion, even when they are still. He frequently plays with perspectives, disrupting how we believe we are 'seeing' the film. For example, the artist's canvas is revealed to be the hide of a cow in *Spotting a Cow* (*Het Scheppen Van Een Koe*, 1983) and the complete overturning of reality in *Tip Top* (1984) and *Sunny Side Up* (*Spiegeleiland*, 1985). His films are often philosophical, and usually present a fairly bleak worldview, although never at the expense of humour. In *The Same Old Story* (*Une*

Histoire Comme Une Autre, 1981), a Chinese box style story ends with the viewer possibly about to repeat the same mistakes as the character we have just watched. *Home on the Rails (Het Treinhusje,* 1981) set during the expansion of the American West, presents us with an old couple through whose home the railway runs. Its expansion eventually ruins their livelihood, and provides them with a means of ending it all.

Driessen insists that his work contains 'no observations about life and people'. But certainly some of the stories that he tells could be seen to be commenting upon certain aspects of human nature, whether cloaked in fantasy or not. The character in *The Writer* (1985) is shown to wield his power of life and death over his characters with nearly as much arbitrariness as the skeletal figure of Death that stalks around the outskirts of his life and the story he is writing.

Possibly Driessen's finest cartoon is a commentary on the dangers of conformity. *Elbowing (Jeu Des Coudes,* 1979) features a group of grim-faced men in a line, each of whom takes turns in elbowing the next person to them. The result each time is that the last person is elbowed over an unseen precipice and the line all moves up one and begins again. Disrupting this internecine game is a non-conformist. Each time his turn comes, he breaks up the flow by being out of place or juggling or generally fooling around. However, he always returns to the line at last, to continue the elbowing. When his turn at the end of the line comes, he simply walks off. Surprised, the penultimate person nudges the one next to him to report. The nudge is passed back up the line to the first of the group, who is, to his horror, elbowed off the other end of the precipice.

While Driessen may not intend his films to reflect upon human nature, it is difficult not to find such reflections in them. The fact that he does not lecture, but engages his audience in an imaginary world where we might recognise ourselves, counts much in his favour. His active questioning of the creative process and accepted filmic language adds another layer to his animation and to the pleasure of viewing them. And they are also very funny.

Bob Godfrey

Bob Godfrey occupies that special place in a certain generation's heart that also holds dear Oliver Postgate. Godfrey was the creator of three children's programmes fondly remembered by thirtysomethings: *Roobarb*, *Noah and Nelly* and *Henry's Cat*. But, unlike Postgate, Godfrey's canon is not confined to children's television.

Born in Horse Shoe Bend, West Maitland, Australia on 27 May 1922, Godfrey grew up in London. It was here that he learned animation, working for the Larkins studio. It had been one of two animation studios founded in the UK in 1940, the other being Halas & Batchelor. Both studios had worked throughout the war producing educational and propaganda films, mainly working on commissions from various government departments. Bill Larkins along with Peter Sachs and Denys Gilpin produced graphically revolutionary animation, arguably before UPA had begun rewriting the rulebook with their modernist backgrounds.

During Godfrey's spare time at Larkins, he worked with Keith Learner to make *Watch the Birdie* (1954). In the same year he founded Biographic Films with Learner, Vera Linnecar and Nancy Hanna. The company was established to make commissioned work only, but its success meant that Godfrey was able to make more personal films. The first, *Polygamous Polonius* (1959) unveiled the themes that would characterise many of his animated films: sex and the absurd (and often both at once – no one seems able to pin down the vaguely melancholic absurdity of sex better than Godfrey). His work at Biographic feels closely aligned to the work of Richard Lester, for whom he produced animated inserts for TV shows such as Spike Milligan's *A Show Called Fred* (1958) and Michael Bentine's *It's a Square World* (1963). It's particularly strong when you compare Lester's *The Running, Jumping and Standing Still Film* (1959) with Godfrey's *Alf, Bill And Fred* (1964), which features a man, a dog and a duck who enjoy bouncing up and down for no reason other than Godfrey wants to make us laugh. The cartoon's music, supplied by cinema pianist Arthur Dulay, adds the final touch.

Anyway, Godfrey followed *Polonius* with the *Do It Yourself Cartoon Kit* (1963), which mercilessly guyed the conventions of animation in a style that predates the *Monty Python* animations of Terry Gilliam. Coincidentally, a pre-Python Gilliam had turned up at Godfrey's around 1968 looking for work. The animators were so impressed by his portfolio that Godfrey, fearing he might cause unrest, told him to 'bugger off'.

After making *The Rise and Fall of Emily Sprod* (1964), Godfrey parted ways with his partners and set up a new studio. It was with this new company that Godfrey entered the most rewarding part of his career. *Two off the Cuff* (1967) saw a more sophisticated sense of humour at work. *Henry 9 'til 5* (1970) continued in this vein but allowed Godfrey's flights of fancy and obsession with sex to return. It tells of Henry, a 'little man' who passes the time at his humdrum job by fantasising about sex. These erotic daydreams become increasingly complex and absurd. Henry returns home at the end of the day to his wife (unseen but vocally represented as voluptuous and eager for sexual activity). Needless to say, Henry replies that he is unable to comply as he has had a hard day at the office. *Kama Sutra Rides Again* (1971) takes the theme further, with a middle-aged suburban couple's attempts at sexual reawakening encompassing increasingly bizarre positions.

Great (1975) was Godfrey's most ambitious feature to date. It is a half-hour-long musical celebrating the achievements of Victorian engineer Isambard Kingdom Brunel. Made piecemeal and financed by money from commercials, the studio's faith paid off when it won an Oscar.

Godfrey continued to explore sexual themes with *Instant Sex* (1979) and *Bio-Woman* (1981). He also collaborated with Croatian animator Zlatko Grgic for *Lutka Snova* aka *Dream Doll* (1979), in which another 'little man' falls in love with an inflatable sex doll. It ends with him borne aloft by flocks of the dolls in a deliberate parody of Disney's *Peter Pan*. Godfrey also made idiosyncratic films for Switzerland's 500th anniversary (*Happy Birthday, Switzerland*) and the French Revolution (*Coming Soon! Revolution*). There was also an ill-fated piece financed by the Millennium Commission, detailing 2000 years of human endeavour in ten minutes.

While the Godfrey studio has continued to produce independent work (including animating the work of *The Guardian*'s satirical cartoonist, Steve Bell), they have become more famous for their children's TV series for the BBC. *Roobarb* is probably the most anarchic and most fondly remembered. Telling of the antics of an egotistical green dog (Roobarb) and a sarcastic pink cat (Custard), the five-minute-long episodes managed to contain enough of Godfrey's wit and flights of fancy to retain their individuality. *Roobarb* was written by Grange Calveley, voiced by Richard Briers and animated in a deliberately old-fashioned 'tremulant' style (i.e., the pictures wobbled as if viewing a child's flick book).In *Noah and Nelly* (also narrated by Briers and written by Calveley) the characters travel to strange new lands in an ark on wheels. Rather than having animals 'two by two', each creature had two heads (like Dr Dolittle's Pushmipullyu). *Henry's Cat* also had flights of fancy, but was markedly less crazed than *Roobarb*. It was written by Godfrey's collaborator on many projects (including *Polonius*, *Alf* and *Kama Sutra*), Stan Hayward, another Australian émigré.

Godfrey has been compared to Alfred Jarry and Rabelais.While these comparisons stand, time has revealed him to be equally successful whether in satirising social/sexual mores or in providing more quietly subversive fare.

Aardman Animation

Aardman's success in the field of stop-motion animation has been something of an anomaly. Putting aside Ray Harryhausen's mythological tormentors of live actors, in films such as *Jason and the Argonauts* and *Clash of the Titans*, there had been precious few fully stop-motion animated films that had been successful at the box office. The one major exception was the truly quirky Tim Burton's *The Nightmare Before Christmas* (1993). At this point in animated cinema, only Pixar's brand of computer-generated events (*Toy Story*, *A Bug's Life*) were succeeding at the box office, and they were currently suffering, like most live-action studios, from sequelitis (*Toy Story 2*). Disney, meanwhile, were showing off CGI effects for *Dinosaur* (2000) in a plot lifted from Don Bluth's cel-animated *The Land Before Time* (1988) and the retrogressive and thoroughly ill-advised *Fantasia 2000* (1999). Meanwhile, Don Bluth, who had branched out into computer-generated animation for the space opera *Titan AE* (2000) had been completely shafted by Twentieth Century Fox, who not only gave the film very little publicity, but also closed down Bluth's animation studio upon the film's release.

Aardman was founded in 1972 in Bristol. Its founders, Peter Lord and David Sproxton, had first met at secondary school where they both worked on a short animation which they submitted to the BBC. A children's producer commissioned the two teenagers to produce short pieces of animation for the children's art programme *Vision On*. Their first was a piece of cel animation featuring an inept superhero called Aardman. They named the company in honour of their first big break and created Morph, a small 'claymation' (animated clay or, more often, Plasticine) figure who could change shape at will. Originally planned for *Vision On*, Morph first appeared in 1976, as part of its successor *Take Hart*. Morph soon got his own series of five-minute-long adventures, *The Amazing Adventures of Morph*, which proved popular with children and adults alike.

Sproxton and Lord continued to produce claymation work for both the BBC and Channel 4, but were keen not to be seen just as animators for children's programmes. Their later work, such as *Animated Conversations* (1978, BBC, two episodes) and *Conversation Pieces* (1982, C4, five episodes), is marked by its fine attention to character detail. Their shorts for these two series featured unscripted dialogue recorded from people's daily lives (a door-to-door salesman in *Sales Pitch*, a reformed burglar in *Going Equipped*). The claymation characters became theirmouth-pieces, with great attention paid to rendering every facial and physical nuance. This rendering of ordinary lives made Aardman a successor to British cinema's heritage of social realism and the documentary tradition.

Nick Park

Adding to Lord and Sproxton's achievements has been Nick Park, who joined Aardman in 1985. Another animator who had become interested in the format as a child, he also had dreams of becoming a comic strip artist. He graduated from Sheffield Art School and went on to the National Film and Television School in Beaconsfield.

His graduate film, *A Grand Day Out*, which was still uncompleted by the time he joined Aardman, was the first of his films featuring the characters Wallace and Gromit, the cheese-obsessed inventor and his smart dog. Upon completion, his next film was part of Sproxton and Lord's *Lip Synch* series for Channel 4 (1989). The short *Creature Comforts* followed the same technique as the likes of *Going Equipped* but, instead of humans, the claymation consisted of animals in a zoo speaking the words of humans, mainly senior citizens in a retirement home and children discussing animals in the zoo. The high point was supplied by a Brazilian student (portrayed as a jagnar) who hated pretty much everything about Britain.

By this time, *A Grand Day Out* had also been completed. Both featured Park's trademarks: characters with coat hanger-wide mouths and a nice sense of background detail. Both films were on the Oscar shortlist for best animated feature and *Creature Comforts* won. Its success and popularity led to many repeat showings on Channel 4 and a similarly themed series of adverts for British Gas. Recently, Park has returned to the idea for a series of shorter slots on ITV 1. Park and Aardman's success came particularly from the popularity of Wallace and Gromit. The beautifully observed details of their relationship give the characters an immediate depth and familiarity. The humour comes from Wallace's Heath-Robinson-style labour-saving devices (that usually backfire) to Gromit's long-suffering nature and his usually pained facial expressions.

Park's second Wallace and Gromit feature *The Wrong Trousers* (1993) is arguably the best of the three. On

Gromit's birthday, Wallace tactlessly presents him with a pair of robotic 'techno-trousers' (bought cheap from NASA) which have been re-engineered to take Gromit for 'walkies'. The trousers and Wallace's technical know-how are then exploited by a criminal mastermind penguin who usurps Gromit's place in the house and uses the trousers (with Wallace trapped in them) to pull off a spectacular diamond theft. A climactic train chase ensues (on a model railway inside the house) and Gromit succeeds in capturing the penguin. The trousers end up in the dustbin but walk off into the sunset. In *The Wrong Trousers* the animation and timing are topnotch. Fleshed out with ingenious little touches (the penguin replacing Gromit's bone wallpaper with fish wallpaper, the planning of the robbery, with the penguin gliding through the air on the end of a retractable tape measure, its final capture in a milk-bottle), *The Wrong Trousers* never hits a wrong note. It deservedly won an Oscar. Park's next outing for the duo was *A Close Shave* (1995), which also won the Oscar for animation. In this instalment, the duo find themselves up against sheep rustling and the evil plans of a robotic dog and a nicely played climax which replays the end of *The Terminator*.

Needless to say, when Hollywood came knocking the first suggestion was a Wallace and Gromit movie.

The main Hollywood interest came from DreamWorks, the company founded by Steven Spielberg, David Geffen and Jeffrey Katzenberg. The idea that Aardman pitched was *The Great Escape* but with chickens. DreamWorks and Aardman, although an unlikely pairing, paid off (in 1999, they announced that they would co-produce a further four features). Aardman's film *Chicken Run* (2000) was fully backed by DreamWorks and their publicity machine. Directed by Nick Park and Peter Lord, it garnered star voices like Mel Gibson and Jane Horrocks. Its success at the box office was further aided by the fact that Aardman knew both that character is as deeply important to bringing animated characters to life as the animation, and that children don't need to be talked down to. Thus, both adults and children were attracted to the film. Despite the professional animation and good humour and invention that has gone into *Chicken Run*, it feels a little too polished. There are certainly no shortage of exciting and funny moments but there is a sense that there is a little piece of its soul missing. But, these are small quibbles compared to the fact that so much of Aardman is on screen: Park's characters are all neatly observed individuals and the gadgets on display (the farmer's pie-making machine and the chickens' plane) could have almost have been supplied from Wallace's workshop. If you have any interest in how traditional animation can continue to progress, you should see it and marvel that it ever got made in the first place.

Eastern Europe

'I prefer objects which, to my way of thinking, have their own interior life.'

Jan Švankmajer

Cinema in most East European countries was state-funded and thus dependent upon each country's political leadership. The state controlled all areas of cinema, including exhibition and theatres. With animation's appeal to children, most output was aimed at younger viewers. As ideological control eased, animators were allowed to explore different styles and themes. Such relaxation varied from country to country, but in most cases, animation was then divided between functional and prestigious films. Prestigious animation was made by a select few who could blaze their own trail. That said, no animator was ever granted complete artistic control and many films were still suppressed due to the supposed ideological danger they posed. As the dominant social realism frowned upon references or inspiration drawn from the Western avant-garde movements, many animators turned to the folksongs and legends of their countries for their ideas.

Animation themes varied from country to country and, as with the other areas considered in this book, to give a thorough picture would prove impossible. Below are just a few of the animators who, despite censorship, turned the restrictions to their advantage and have produced influential and lasting works of art.

Jirí Trnka

Born in Pilsen in 1912, Trnka studied art under one of the great puppeteers, Josef Skupa. Skupa also made Trnka his assistant and taught him how to carve wooden puppets. Czech puppet theatre had a centuries-old tradition of dissent and originated as a cheaper substitute to ordinary theatre. After the First World War many new puppet theatres arose, and were prepared to tackle any genre. It was also in Czechoslovakia that the puppet theatre most easily made the leap into cinema.

Trnka also worked as a scene designer for avant-garde director Jir Frejka but his love for puppet theatre continued and he founded the Wooden Theatre. The venture did not last long and, between 1936 and 1945 he established a reputation as a leading figure in book illustration and stage design. During this period he continued to make puppets for his own amusement.

His opportunity to learn film animation came when Czechoslovakia was liberated at the end of the Second World War. The film industry was nationalised and Trnka was asked to head a team of artists, calling themselves the Trick Brothers, in a project to inject new talent into film animation. His first films, such as his debut, *Grandfather Planted a Beet* used only cel animation. The colourful *The Animals and the Brigands* (*Zvířátka A Petrovští*, 1946) won a prize at the first Cannes film festival, Trnka's first real recognition outside his homeland. In contrast, *The Springer and the SS* (*Pérák A SS* also 1946), a tale of a chimney sweep's fight against the Nazis, was told in stark black and white. It was with *The Gift* (*Dárek*, 1946), a semi-surreal satire on the middle classes, that he confirmed his reputation as an innovator in animation and several critics considered him to be Europe's first serious challenger to the already all-pervasive Disney.

In 1947, he left Trick Brothers and was allocated studio space in an old villa near the centre of Prague. It was here that he established the Prague Puppet Film Studio which, after his death in 1969, was renamed the Jiří Trnka Puppet Studio.

His first independent work, *The Czech Year* (*Špalíček*, 1947) documented Czech customs throughout the changing seasons. It showed his deep affection for nature and popular culture and revealed a modest but still powerful lyricism. It was also his first film to demonstrate his expert handling of puppetry in stop-motion animation. His next film, *The Emperor's Nightingale* (*Císaruv Slavík*, 1948) was based on a story by Hans Christian Andersen. While the porcelain features of his puppets and the grandeur of the setting in the imperial palace were far removed from the earthy Bohemian peasants in *The Czech Year*, the treatment of the subject was ironic, showing such splendour as ridiculously complex in comparison with the simplicity of nature. The fairy-tale theme was one that he would return to for his third film *Prince Bayaya* (*Bajaja*, 1950) and seven years later, he would make arguably his finest statement on how such classical stories could be represented by such simple tools as puppets in *Old Czech Legends* (*Staré Povesti Ceské*, 1957).

His adaptations of more fixed authorial voices were considered less satisfactory and, while his puppet animation was still enjoyed by many, his films of Jaroslav Hayek's *The Good Soldier Schweik* (*Dobry Voják Švejk*, 1955) and Shakespeare's *Midsummer Night's Dream* (*Sen Noci Svatojánské*, 1959) met with criticism about his excessive mannerism.

While other filmmakers struggled to represent all emotions upon their puppets (often keeping vast files of facial expressions ready to be superimposed upon the puppets' heads), Trnka treated the puppets' faces as theatrical masks. The face remained fixed throughout the film. Trnka used framing and lighting to suggest changes of emotion, both externally and internally, and the drama itself lent expression to their movements.

Nowhere can this be seen as more effective than in Trnka's last film: *The Hand* (*Ruka*, 1965). By this point, Trnka had become desperately pessimistic in his outlook. Both of his two previous films: *The Passion* (*Vášen*, 1962) and *The Cybernetic Grandmother* (*Kybernetická Babicka*, 1962) presented bleak viewpoints of the younger generation and of modern technology. In *The Hand*, a potter is continually badgered by a giant white-gloved Hand (Trnka's own) to make a sculpture of a hand instead of the pots that he makes. The potter continually ejects the Hand from his apartment, but never before the Hand has once again broken the pot in which the potter's beloved plant grows. Each time the Hand arrives it offers the potter some reward for making the Hand: a television (which continually shows great hands in history), chocolates, vast sums of money. When the potter refuses once too often, the Hand tries to crush him then lures him to a cage. Here, the potter is forced to create the sculpture of the Hand and is rewarded with laurels and medals. Tearing these off, the potter manages to escape back to his apartment and boards up the door and window. He places his pot plant on top of the wardrobe and, attempting to board this up also, dislodges the pot which falls onto his head and kills him. The Hand arrives. Shocked to find the potter dead, it gives him a funeral with full honours.

Beginning quite playfully, *The Hand* becomes swiftly darker and darker. An enraged hymn to artistic freedom, it can be seen to be attacking both state-funded censorship and how big money co-opts and dilutes the arts. Trnka's animation is both graceful and disturbing. The puppet of the potter, with its eyes always fixed on the middle distance with an undefined expression, suggests that the external struggle with the Hand is not the only struggle that is going on. Its enigmatic little smile, so often hidden during the film as its head droops, is revealed once more in death, but the funeral preparations suggest that the potter will be remembered in death for his sculpture of the Hand, rather than his own more personal work.

After *The Hand*, Trnka was unable to work further due to a heart condition. He died in 1969.

Yuri Norstein

*'An art where we feel we understand in general but can't
fully explain it; that is the strength of art. There must
always be secrets in art.'*

Yuri Norstein

Beginning his career in animation with 1968's *25th October
– The First Day*, Yuri Norstein's films often have their
origins in Russian folk tales. But beneath the anthropomorphism of *The Heron and the Crane* (1974) and *The
Hedgehog in the Fog* (1975) runs an undercurrent of melancholy that belies more literary influences. Norstein
worked on an adaptation of Nikolai Gogol's *The Overcoat*
for over ten years. Funding difficulties and an acrimonious
dispute which resulted in him being evicted from his
studio at Soyuzmultfilm meant the production was
delayed for eight years (both these obstacles were resolved
in 1994).

Usually working with a very small crew, Norstein
frequently employs a multiplane camera. This technique,
patented by Disney in the 1930s, is composed of many
layers, usually of glass. Upon these are painted objects and
backgrounds through which the animated figures 'pass'.
Although far more labour-intensive than the standard
'two-plane' animation, multiplane gives a remarkable illusion of depth to the film. One need look no further than
the tree that the hedgehog bumps into in *The Hedgehog in
the Fog*, to be struck by how effectively Norstein utilises
this method. Norstein's perfectionism and attention to
every detail in his films also means that he works mainly

in 'straight-ahead' animation, eschewing in-betweening in favour of animating each frame one by one.

Briefly, *The Hedgehog in the Fog*'s story is this: Hedgehog goes to visit his friend, a bear cub, who lives across the woods. He is followed by an owl whose predatory presence goes unnoticed. Reaching a valley filled with fog, he sees a horse, but it is soon swallowed up. Faltering, the hedgehog becomes increasingly panicked by half-glimpsed creatures. Trying to run, he falls into the river where he is saved by a passing catfish. He finally arrives at Bear's place, he scolds Hedgehog for being late. Hedgehog remembers the horse and wonders whether it will suffocate if it lays down in the fog.

Hedgehog's final thought is not atypical of this charming but melancholy little film. As befits a creature who has plenty of natural predators, Hedgehog's general demeanour is irredeemably morbid. Floating on his back in the river he says to himself 'I'm soaked – I'll drown soon.' However, the dangers that he imagines never turn out to be fatal. The owl seems more concerned with amusing himself with the echo of his voice in a well than in devouring the hedgehog and the dangers in the fog are more products of Hedgehog's imagination than truly threatening – a bat doesn't acknowledge his existence and a dog is floppy and eager to help. Bear himself is a fussy, podgy character whose scolding hides a deep-felt concern for his friend's well-being. In an industry that thrives on lazy anthropomorphism, Norstein's character's have genuine human qualities without departing entirely from their animal natures.

Norstein's last completed work *Tale of Tales* (1979) was

voted best animated feature by film critics in 1984. It is an impressive confluence of his work to date and his recollections of a childhood in Russia during the Second World War. Combining various animation techniques and focusing upon the wolf cub of a traditional Russian lullaby exploring a deserted country house, *Tale of Tales* has been favourably compared to Tarkovsky's *Mirror* in its use of imagery and time shifts. Its seemingly random string of repeating images (a baby at its mother's breast, men heading off to war, a boy imagining befriending birds in the snow) and uses of various sources of light (a streetlamp beneath which lovers dance, a remembered fireplace in a deserted house, a portal of light leading to the past) make *Tale of Tales* a stream of emotional impressions far removed from that derived from a linear narrative.

Norstein's films remain a well-kept secret within the animation community, mainly due to a scarcity of available prints. They are certainly worth tracking down, as his craftsmanship is a rare thing in these days of CGI. Far from being obscure, his work is accessible and beautiful to watch, forming a bridge between more 'art-house' work by the likes of the Brothers Quay and more mainstream animation, particularly early Disney.

Jan Švankmajer

Born in Prague in 1934, Švankmajer trained at the Institute of Industrial Arts between 1950 and 1954 and then went on to the Fine Arts Academy. He worked with several theatre companies in Prague, including the Theatre of Masks and the Black Theatre. But it was working with the Lanterna Magika Puppet Theatre where his interest in film first began. His first film *The Last Trick* (*Poslední Trik Pana Schwarcewalldea A Pana Edgara*, 1964) detailed a duel between two magicians and it displayed his expertise with puppets as the duo commit various acts of violence upon each other. Also present from the start was his vicious sense of humour. A similar feat would be exhibited with the puppet protagonists in *The Lych House, The Coffin Factory* (*Rakvičkárna*, 1966) as Punch attempts to extract a larger sum of money from Joey (a traditional puppet, similar in costume to that of Harlequin) than he intends to pay for Punch's guinea pig. Both puppets fall into a vicious cycle of violence and premature burial, eventually drawing the puppeteer into their attacks with hammers and nails. Finally laying waste to themselves and the set around them, the guinea pig wanders off, the only survivor of their greed. Aided by his regular composer Zdanek Liska, Švankmajer pulls off moments of genuine eeriness and black humour amongst the episodes of the duel. Newspaper photographs come to life on the walls in the Harlequin's house and the repetitious nature of the fight is ironically commented upon when the film switches from the actions of its protagonists to shots of advertisements for people, hammers and coffins.

Characters locked in a repetitive cycle would continually reappear throughout Švankmajer's work with varying levels of success. In *Et Cetera* (1966), it is the film's *raison d'être*. It is at its most trying in his feature-length adaptation of *Faust* where Faust's manservant continually summons and banishes a devil from Hell. At its best, it can be genuinely heartbreaking, as with the little girl doomed to return to the haunted cellar in *Down to the Cellar* (*Do Pivince,* 1982).

Švankmajer remains a member of the Czech Surrealist Group which he joined in 1970. Many of its members also work on his films, including his wife, artist Eva Švankmajerova and the animator Bedrich Glasser. Švankmajer's own work continues to convey the dreamlike nature of much of the best Surrealist work. Unlike many animators, he continues to work in different techniques, mixing live action, drawn animation, puppets, trick photography and 'claymation', often in the same film.

In 1972, Švankmajer's post-production alterations to *Leonardo's Diary* (*Leonardův Denik*) combined animations of Leonardo Da Vinci's sketches with references to daily life under Soviet control (Czechoslovakia was invaded in 1968), upsetting those in charge. He was 'forced to rest from the cinema' for seven years, finally returning in 1979 with the gothic *Castle of Otranto* (*Otranský Zánek*). His commentaries on life seem no less acidic for his rest. 1982's *Dimensions of Dialogue* (*Moznosti Dialogu*) depicts three different scenarios where breakdown of communication leads to either destruction or monotone conformity. *Virile Games* (*Mužné Bry*, 1988) depicts football as a battlefield, where points are scored for killing members of the opposing team (the clay 'press-out' heads of the footballers are subjected to particularly nasty surrealist violence: one is inflated till it bursts, another has a model train driven through its eye sockets, etc.). His only openly political work, *The Death of Stalinism in Bohemia* (1990), his first after the 'death' of communism, provided a brief history of Czechoslovakia since the Second World War in a startling mixture of documentary footage, stop-motion and montage.

His post-censorship return also saw Švankmajer renew his interest in the works of Lewis Carroll. Whereas *Jabberwocky* (1971) had used the recited poem for a stop-motion elegy on the passing of childhood, his adaptation of *Alice's Adventures in Wonderland: Neco Z Alenky* (*Alice*, 1987) served both as a reclamation of the darker aspects of Carroll's novel from the saccharine adaptations by the likes of Disney and Hanna-Barbera and a handy recapitulation of Švankmajer's earlier works which were finally gaining attention outside of Eastern Europe. To summarise the whole film here would be lengthy and could never do it justice, but images persist: The caterpillar realised as an old sock, sat on a darning mushroom while a needle sews its eyes shut so it can sleep. The skeletally mismatched animals trapping Alice in the White Rabbit's house (children's building blocks outside, dung, straw and chicken wire inside). The White Rabbit himself, a real stuffed rabbit, continually leaking sawdust. In the most disturbing sequence, Alice drinks a substance that turns her into a doll before being caught by a gang of skeletally hybrid animals who force her to walk the plank into a milky substance. This substance makes her grow again, but *as the doll*, which the animals then drag to and imprison in a larder where bread sprouts nails and meat runs amok. Alice, her eyes switching madly through the doll's sockets, finally breaks free by splitting the doll open, like a butterfly escaping a pupa case.

Recently Švankmajer has worked more closely in live action films although they contain elements of animation.

His last animated short, *Jídlo* (*Food*, 1992) was a mixture of live-action and pixilated footage revolving around automation, cannibalism and bad restaurant service. Since then he has focused on full-length films: *Faust* (*Lekce Faust*, 1992), *Conspirators of Pleasure* (*Spiklenci Slasti*, 1996) and *Little Otek*, (*Otesánek*, 2000). In *Faust* he paid tribute to the Czech puppet tradition in which he trained and suggested that, with the right circumstances we could all be Faust. *Conspirators* shares as melancholic a view of mankind's obsessive search for erotic satisfaction as the works of Bob Godfrey. *Little Otek* was a grim little fable about the havoc the voracious appetite of a wooden child wreaks on a Czech suburb. While all three films are predominantly live-action, they contain enough animation, wit and surreal images to show, should anyone doubt it, that Švankmajer still has plenty of tricks up his sleeve.

Quay Brothers

Stephen and Timothy Quay were born in Philadelphia on 17 June 1947. With the exception of a brief stay in Amsterdam, they have lived and worked in London since 1978. On seeing their work for the first time, one could be forgiven for thinking that they are European, perhaps from the Czech Republic like Jan Švankmajer, one of their major influences. Their work is characterised by a dream-like atmosphere where the smallest object or movement is imbued with an intense but elusive significance. Like Švankmajer, their animation has the ability not so much to give life to objects but to locate the lives of the objects. Having attended the Royal College of Art in 1969, they made several amateur animated films in the three proceeding years. But their first real achievement in animation was *Nocturna Artificialia* (1979). It was produced by Keith Griffiths, who became their regular collaborator (and also helped bring Švankmajer's work to British audiences). Although flawed, *Nocturna Artificialia* introduces many of the brothers' strengths: the painstakingly designed interiors and typography, the claustrophobic atmosphere and lighting, and the stop-motion puppetry. Indeed, the motion of the puppets is almost secondary in importance to their pauses, hinting at an inner life that dates from some unknowable past history. Their frequent use of children's dolls, screws, dust, etc. in their films can be seen as further representations of the uncanny in their work, being things that are familiar to the viewer and yet rendered alien by their reanimation. The Quay's resistance to traditional narrative forms allows the audience to draw their own meanings from the ambiguous little worlds that they are shown.

As well as their films appearing to be European, the Quays have also drawn much of their inspiration from European culture (and particularly Middle European). Their second film *Ein Brudermord* (1981) was based on a piece by Franz Kafka. Their series of 'animated documentaries' were similarly inspired. *The Eternal Day of Michel De Gelderode 1898–1962* (1981) related to the eponymous Flemish playwright. *Leos Janácek: Intimate Excursions* (1983) quoted extracts from the diary and music of the Czech composer. *Igor – The Paris Years Chez Pleyel* (1983), featured puppets of Igor Stravinsky, Jean Cocteau and Vladimir Mayakovsky and their thoughts and deeds in the Paris of the 1920s. The brothers paid tribute in *The Cabinet of Jan Švankmajer – Prague's Alchemist of Film* (1984). It acknowledged one of Švankmajer's influences, Giuseppe Arcimboldo, by rendering Švankmajer's puppet as a combination of film equipment and drawing instruments. Utilising several pieces of music by Švankmajer's regular composer Ždenek Liska, the film featured geometrically complex sets that would have given M C Escher pause for thought. It also demonstrates (but never clearly explains) various elements of animation – most notably when Švankmajer and his new apprentice film a ball bouncing down a staircase. As they film it, the ball freezes in mid-air for one shot, then lands on a step for the next.

Perhaps their finest film to date is *Street of Crocodiles* (1986), based on the collection of pseudo-autobiographical stories by Polish author Bruno Schulz. Here is a complete world on display, as if in a museum. The sliding glass doors that close off various cases to the lead puppet make this analogy abundantly clear. If one has read the stories (published in a single volume with *The Sanatorium Under the Sign of the Hourglass* by Picador in 1988) then certain aspects of the film become clear (such as the gentlemen's outfitter who deals in under-the-counter pornography), but, as with all of the brothers' films, this is not a necessity. What matters is that one is drawn into this self-contained world, and that all objects have equal importance, equal resonance. A redheaded character is released into this world and his wanderings through it form the film (one can hardly use the word 'narrative') that we see, as if dreaming with our eyes open (a comment that has been applied to cinema as a whole long before now). Screws unscrew themselves, dust shifts, wires and pulleys move with no immediate design behind their actions. Children's dolls, their eye-sockets lit from within, encircle the redheaded figure and briefly remove his head. There is also a running motif of scissors and cutting, as if freedom is being granted but with it comes certain censorships.

The brothers followed this with *Little Songs of the Chief Officer of Hunar Louse,* or *This Unnameable Little Broom Tableau II* (1985) which was based on *The Epic of Gilgamesh.* It takes some work to actually place the film within that context, even though they make clear the reference within the film's title.

More recently, the Quays have produced their first live-action film *Institute Benjamenta or This Dream People Call Human Life* (1995), starring Alice Krige and Mark Rylance. It was based on *Jakob Von Gunten* (1908) by the Swiss writer Robert Walser, whose writings had also inspired *The Comb* (1990). Other than 'the gallery' – a place that Krige's character can see from the window of her room, there is little animation. It moves at an almost painfully stately pace, with every sentence uttered heavy with intention. Its use of lighting and décor make it eerily beautiful to look at but the live action seems dreadfully handicapping. While certain moments are fascinating, it feels more glacial than even they might have wished for.

Since *Benjamenta,* they have worked on several collaborations: *In Absentia* (2000) with Karlheinz Stockhausen, and two dance videos for the Royal Canadian Ballet: *Duet* (2000) and *The Sandman* (2001). They created a dream sequence for Julie Taymor's film *Frida* (2002), on the life of Frida Kahlo, and the short film *The Phantom Museum*

(2002). This portrayed the life of exhibits belonging to Sir Henry Wellcome's Medical Collection 'after the last visitor has left the gallery', and was shown on a loop as part of the British Museum's 2003 exhibition *Medicine Man: The Forgotten Museum of Henry Wellcome*.

Admittedly sometimes the brothers' work can feel too obscure, such as with *Rehearsals for Extinct Anatomies* (1988) or *The Comb*, but the often discomfiting pleasure derived from their intense visual style soon allays any feeling that one is sitting in on a private coded conversation between two uniquely matched minds.

And just in case you were wondering why I haven't mentioned the videos for the nu-metal band Tool, they were directed by Quay-wannabe Fred Stuhr, interesting though they were. (The Brothers did, however, create videos for bands such as His Name Is Alive and Sparkle-horse.)

Anime – A Brief Introduction

Animation had been produced in Japan on a small-scale since the 1930s. The man who made a difference to this was Osamu Tezuka who helped to make it the multi-million dollar industry that it has become today. His roughly drawn style of characters with saucer eyes became the most recognizable trait of Japanese animation.

Tezuka started out as a graphic artist and moved naturally into animation as a way of furthering his ambitions. His first film as an animation director was *Saiyu-ki* (1960) which was a complex tale about Alakazam, a monkey with magical powers. Probably his most important contribution to making Japan a major player in animation was *Astro Boy* (*Tetsuan-Atoma*). He began the series in 1963 and it was soon redubbed into several other languages, including English and distributed around the world. Subtly reworking *Pinocchio* for the space age, *Astro Boy* was a robot boy created by Dr Tenma to replace the real son he had lost. The robot is later sold and, in righting wrongs and many good deeds, becomes a super hero. *Astro Boy* was fast, fun and cheaply produced. Its success led to the creation of other low-budget series such as *Speed Racer* and the much-cherished *Battle of the Planets*.

Tezuka's success led to the flowering of an industry

which saw its greatest popularity in the West arise around 1987. As the home video market boomed, access to the more cultish manga anime became easier. The accusations levelled at much of the material for its explicitly violent and sexual content came more from the different cultural backgrounds between east and west rather than any desire that the Japanese harboured to warp the minds of western youth.

The success of manga overseas was also paved by the theatrical release of *Akira* (1988, director Katsuhiro Otamo) and the video release of the controversial *Urotsukidōji – Legend of the Overfiend* (1989, director Hideki Takayama) which featured graphic and colourful possessions plus demons with the usual lust for Japanese schoolgirls. *Akira*, directed by Katsuhiro Otamo, the author of the manga on which the film was based, remains particularly impressive, even up to its warped *2001 – A Space Odyssey*-style conclusion. Others, such as *Ghost In the Shell* (1989–90, director Oshii Mamoru), and *Appleseed* (1988–91, director Kazuyoshi Katayama) proved equally popular.

To separate anime and manga entirely is not an easy task. Manga itself is the name for the graphic serial novels which form a huge publishing industry in Japan. Unlike most comic books in the West, they are treated not as a disposable medium but with, say, the same seriousness that Art Spiegelman's *Maus* was approached with in the West. Given that they are usually published in instalments over a long period, their storylines are often extremely complex, with many sub-plots and digressions along the way (perhaps a closer comparison with Western comics would be David Sims' epic *Cerebus the Aardvark*). Anime, while not exclusively adapting manga for the screen, is generally seen in Japan as being another facet of manga, albeit manga that moves. One criticism of anime is that the acting of the characters is reduced to stylised facial expressions rather than genuine emotion – this itself is a reflection of the symbolic expression of emotions in comics as a whole – a picture is worth a thousand words and the readers can immediately grasp what the character is feeling.

Hayao Miyazaki

In Japan, Miyazaki is as well thought of as, say, Spielberg is in the West. His latest feature, *Spirited Away* (*Sen To Chihiro No Kamikakushi*, 2001) won an Oscar for best animated feature and was released, via Disney, in both a subtitled and dubbed version (directed by Kirk Wise, co-director of *Beauty and the Beast* and *Atlantis: The Lost Empire*). One journalist dubbed Miyazaki, 'the Japanese Disney'. While this epithet has certainly helped attract Western audiences to his work, it's not particularly fair to either animator. While Miyazaki's films aren't as polished as Disney's animation when Walt still supervised, his films certainly have more depth – textually and emotionally.

He was born in the Bunkyo-Ho district of Tokyo. His father and his uncle were both involved in the family aeroplane company, Miyazaki Airplane. His films continue to reflect that formative influence, forever delighting in various forms of flight and flying machines. He had already shown a proficiency at drawing from a young age and harboured ambitions to become a manga artist. At his last year at school, he saw the anime *The Legend of the White Serpent* and resolved to become an animator instead. (Although this has not stopped him since from producing several manga, including *Nausicaä of the Valley of the Wind*, 1982–87, 1990–91, 1993–4, *Miscellaneous Memorandum – The Age of Floatplanes*, 1990 and *Tiger in the Mire*, 1998. He also filmed some of *Nausicaä* in 1984.) After graduating in his early twenties, he got a job at Toei-Cine as an inbetweener. By the time of the TV series *Husle Punch* (*Hassuri Panchi,* 1965–66), he was working as a key animator.

In 1971, he left Toei-Cine along with his close friend, director Ikao Takahata. The two moved to A-Pro, a company which frequently produced work for Tokyo Movie. Here, Miyazaki worked on the development of a TV adaptation of Astrid Lundgren's *Pippi Longstocking*, before the screen rights fell through and, despite his ambitions, he saw two of his own screenplays directed by Takahata. They left in 1974 to join Nippon Animation.

It was in 1978 that Miyazaki finally got his first directing job, making twenty-six episodes of the TV adaptation of Alexander Keys' *The Incredible Tide,* entitled *Future Boy Conan* (*Mirai Shônen Conan*). His other responsibilies for the series included storyboards, layouts, character and scene design. While it contained elements that Miyazaki would develop in his own films (an orphan boy searches for a kidnapped girl in a post-holocaust world), television meant that deadlines and the budget were tight, reining in his more artistic impulses.

Then Tokyo Movie (now renamed Tokyo Movie

Shinsha) offered him a cinema feature to direct. It was a sequel to a rather workmanlike film *The Secret of Mamo* (*Lupin Sansei: Mamo Karano Chousen,* 1978) and, like its predecessor, was to be based on Monkey Punch's manga *Lupin Sansei* (itself based upon Maurice Leblanc's series of novels about Arsène Lupin, the gentleman jewel thief, which had been filmed several times and, during the 1970s, and was also a popular French TV series). Miyazaki's sequel *The Castle of Cagliostro* (*Rupan Sensei: Kariosutoro No Shiro,* 1979), invested the series' characters with greater depth and produced a tightly paced plot. What could have been a by-the-numbers sequel proved to be something far more enjoyable, with adult characters, impressive design and a nice line in wit.

After this success, Miyazaki found himself back directing for TV, including episodes of the *Lupin III* series (1980) and a Sherlock Holmes adaptation. A promising project via Hemdale for a feature based on Winsor McCay's *Little Nemo* and involving French artist Moebius, fell apart amidst much acrimony. It was during this time that Miyazaki began to publish his popular manga *Nausicaä*. Several of its admirers talked Miyazaki into adapting it for the screen. He was reluctant at first; the manga was both complex and unfinished but, with Takahata as producer, he managed to produce a fair adaptation. *Nausicaä of the Valley of the Wind* (*Kaze No Tani No Nausicaä,* 1984) does have faults, especially in its animation and plotting, but as Miyazaki was to prove over and again, his strengths in creating believable other worlds and strong female protagonists didn't fail him here. A brutally cut US version released in 1986 did nobody any favours.

Nausicaä's success in Japan encouraged Miyazaki and Takahata to set up their own animation company, Studio Ghibli. Their first feature was *Laputa: Castle in the Sky* (*Tenku No Shiro Rapyuta*, 1986). It featured two orphans who were pursued by a ramshackle band of air-pirates and worse.

His next film was harder to sell to investors, being a bucolic tale about two girls and a woodland sprite who helps them come to terms with their mother's illness. Eventually *My Neighbour Totoro* (*Tonari No Totoro*, 1988) was pitched, and filmed, as a lighter support movie for Isao Takahata's darker *Grave of the Fireflies* (*Hotaru No Haka*, 1988), a tale of a boy's life and eventual death in postwar Japan.

Miyazaki followed this with *Kiki's Delivery Service* (*Majo No Takkyubin*, 1989) about a trainee witch. By this time, he was also producing his own features along with other Ghibli features, including several of Takahata's projects. He also produced, storyboarded and scripted Yoshifumi Kondo's *Whisper of the Heart* (1995). Kondo was being groomed to take over Miyazaki's place at Ghibli. Tragically, Kondo died before that could happen, aged 47.

Miyazaki next directed *Porco Rosso* (*Kurenai No Buta*, 1992), a film specifically aimed at a grown-up audience which depicted the exploits of a pilot between the wars. For the next five years, his time was taken up with production work and, apart from the short musical film *On Your Mark* (1995), he directed nothing else. Another part of the reason for his absence from the screen was that he had spent much of the intervening years planning *Princess Mononoke* (*Mononoke Hime*, 1997). At the time of planning, he had believed that it would be his last film as a director and was determined to make it his defining cinematic moment. Hardly surprising then that its 135-minute running time is crammed with incident and scenic detail with well-rounded and gracefully animated characters. Its release in the west was greeted positively but not without reservations about the greyscale ending and the lack of a definite villain to destroy. But then, Miyazaki generally resists such easy options, recognising that children are more than capable of grasping plot subtleties such as more open-ended endings, and also that good and evil aren't so easily defined in the real world.

If anything, its follow up *Spirited Away* (*Sen To Chihiro No Kamikakushi*) is even better. Ten year-old Chihiro and parents are moving to a new home. They take a wrong turning and end up in a mysterious town. When the parents eat the still-hot food in a deserted restaurant, they are turned into pigs as night falls. Meanwhile, Chihiro finds an empty bathhouse and meets a boy, Haku, who tells her that this place is where spirits and gods come to relax. In order to save her parents, Chihiro must work there, under the management of large-headed sorceress Yubaba. Haku turns into a dragon as punishment for stealing a seal from Yubaba's twin sister, Zeniba. Zeniba arrives at the bathhouse and turns Yubaba's gigantic baby into a large mouse. Chihiro bathes various creatures, including No-face, a demon who goes on an eating rampage and is only stopped when Chihiro tricks it into eating an emetic. Returning Zeniba's seal, Chihiro is flown back by dragon-Haku. Chihiro recalls being rescued as a child from drowning by Haku, she says his real name and he is turned back. At the bathhouse Chihiro's parents are changed back when she passes a final test.

To those familiar with Miyazaki's previous works, you can gather that here are many of his favourite themes: flight, ecology, tired gods, strong girls and empowerment through labour. The supporting characters are lovingly rendered, from the spider-man Kamaji stoking the furnaces, to the mouse-baby, hovering through the air supported by a miniaturised crow (buzzing like a wasp) and the look of the film (the beautiful blending of architectural styles in the bathhouse, the journey on the amphibious train) completely immerse the viewer in Chihiro's world.

Given that Miyazaki thought *Mononoke* would be his last film, *Spirited Away* is a bonus. It is to be hoped that Miyazaki continues against his expectations, especially as his work continues to prove that, despite CGI prophets, traditional animation can still be a wonderful thing.

Computer Animation

'I think the idea of a traditional story being told using traditional animation is likely a thing of the past.'
Jeffrey Katzenberg of DreamWorks, on *Sinbad*

To say that the history of Pixar animation studio is the history of computer animation is to drastically simplify both. But the fact remains that many of the people who have worked or continue to work at Pixar have been instrumental in the progression of computer graphics to the point where highly successful and popular feature-length animation can be made with computer program. It is something that, until nearly 15 years ago had still looked fairly unlikely. This was, in part, due to Hollywood's continued resistance to computer animation as a part of the filmmaking process. Films that had used computer animation as an important component of the narrative had proved both costly and unpopular. Disney sank around $20 million into Steve Lisberger's *Tron* (1982) (with computer work by John Whitney Jr and Gary Demos of Information International Incorporated or Triple I) and were poorly rewarded for their troubles. A similar lack of profits for Lorimar's *The Last Starfighter* (1984) hardly helped matters. And these were films where the computer imaging was only part of the film.

Most of the earliest fully computer animated films were made by the programs who had designed the graphics programs in order to demonstrate how they operated. One of the first was made by E E Zajac at Bell Telephone Laboratory in 1963 and entitled *Simulation of a Two-Giro Gravity Attitude Control System*. It demonstrated how the attitude of a satellite could be altered as it orbits the Earth. Hardly an event film as Hollywood would see it, but it was one of several such films that made corporations such as General Electric begin to take an interest in computer graphics. Most early computer graphics were Vector graphics which were composed of thin lines, whereas modern graphics are Raster graphics using pixels.

In the late 1960s Ivan Sutherland and Dave Evans, both of whom had helped develop computer graphics programs, were recruited to the University of Utah (UU) to form a computer science program. One of their students was Ed Catmull, who started at UU in 1970. His love of animation found a natural progression in the computer graphics research that was being conducted there. Most of his work at UU covered surface representation, including texture mapping, where realistic 2-D surfaces are applied to 3-D computer images, rather like hanging wallpaper. As UU ran out of funding around 1974, Catmull was made director of the New York Institute of Technology's (NYIT) new Computer Graphics Lab. His employer, Alexander Schure, shared an interest in computer animation and had already established a traditional animation facility at NYIT. As others moved from UU to NYIT, it became the new centre of excellence for developing computer graphics programming. Originally focusing on 2-D animation, Catmull built the 'Tween', a computerised tool which interpolated the in-between frames from one key drawing to the next. NYIT also developed a scan-and-paint system for pencilled artwork. This would later become Disney's CAPS (Computer Animation Production System).

Creation at NYIT was feverish, with many of the students, including Alvy Ray Smith (creator of SuperPaint), working 22 hour shifts. Schure, their financier, made a conventional animated film called *Tubby the Tuba*. It was so bad that it suddenly dawned on them that, while they were technically innovative, they hadn't the creativity to make a movie themselves.

Meanwhile, George Lucas, whose plans to use Triple I for CGI effects in *The Empire Strikes Back* were scuppered by financial disagreements, decided to create his own CGI department within Lucasfilm. For his recruits he went to NYIT. Initially only five went with Lucas, including Catmull, Smith and Ralph Guggenheim. But gradually, the unit at NYIT broke up and more left to join Lucasfilm. Following the embarrassment of *Tubby*, the NYIT recruits were happy to provide the research and development and let Lucas worry about the creative aspect of moviemaking.

In 1976, James Blinn at the Jet Propulsion Laboratory in Pasadena developed a new variation on Catmull's texture mapping. This version, known as Bump Mapping, uses colours to make a surface appear dented or bulging. A monochrome image is used; white areas appear as bulges, black as dents. Shades of grey are represented as smaller bumps depending on the darkness of the shade. He also wrote a paper on creating surfaces that reflect their environment. This is known as environment mapping. Blinn would later join NYIT.

During the 1980s, *the* conference to meet and share ideas about computer graphics and animation was the Association of Computing Machinery's Special Interest Group on Computer Graphics (SIGGRAPH). It had begun in 1973, and started allowing exhibitors in 1976. By 1993, 275 companies would be exhibiting their work. In 1980, Loren Carpenter's film *Vol Libre* was shown, displaying a computer-generated flight through fractal mountains. Carpenter had worked for Boeing Computer Services since 1966 and was hired by Lucasfilm on the strength of *Vol Libre*. For them he created the first renderer, named REYES (Renders Everything You Ever Saw). It would eventually become Renderman, the program that was key to Pixar's success. Carpenter still works for Pixar.

In 1984, John Lasseter, disillusioned at Disney, left to join Lucasfilm. During this time, he worked on his first short film *Andre and Wally B*, which was shown at SIGGRAPH. He was surprised to be asked by someone there what software he had used to make the characters funny.

The special effects at Lucasfilm were handled by Industrial Light & Magic (ILM) and they kept the computer graphics people at arm's length, considering it to be too low resolution for film. The CGI wing split from ILM in 1986 to become Pixar. Lucasfilm would retain access to Pixar's rendering technology. Catmull became president and Smith vice-president. Before Catmull left, he hired two people to maintain a CGI presence at ILM. By the mid-80s, this presence *had become* ILM. Also in 1986, Lasseter's short *Luxo, Jr* premiered at SIGGRAPH. With this short, Lasseter proved that his creative abilities were more than capable of utilising Pixar's R&D, by breathing life, character and humour into two CGI anglepoise lamps.

Lasseter continued to produce short CGI films, including *Tin Toy* (1988), in which can be seen the genesis of the all-conquering *Toy Story*. A small tin one-man band is terrorised by a curious baby whose birthday present he is. Finally diving for safety under the sofa, he is confronted with many of the infant's old toys, all of whom are also cowering in terror. It won an Oscar in 1989, the same year that his film *Knick Knack* (about the envious life of characters in snow globes) premiered.

ILM's success in computer animation is continually seen and felt in films such as *The Abyss* (the water-*Alien*) *Terminator 2* (Robert Patrick morphing into molten metal), and *Jurassic Park* (have a guess). By 1993, IBM, James Cameron, special effects wiz Stan Winston and ILM's visual effects expert Scott Ross had formed Digital Domain. Not to be beaten, ILM joined forces with Silicon Graphics, Inc., to form Joint Environment for Digital Imaging (sigh . . . 'JEDI').

At Pixar, resources were put into developing Renderman, with Pat Hanrahan organising technical details and naming it. Created in 1988, it is a standard for describing 3-D scenes, including objects, light sources, cameras, and atmospheric effects. Once a scene has been created as a Renderman file, it can be rendered on most computer systems. One of its most important components is the use of shaders which are pieces of code to describe surfaces and lighting and atmospheric effects. These ensure that, if you were to slice open the object, the texture would remain the same within (e.g., a 3-D CGI cube of 'wood' cut open would reveal the wood grain running through it).

In 1991, Disney and Pixar announced an agreement to create the first feature-length computer-animated film. The same year, Disney released *Beauty and the Beast*. Here, they used CGI throughout to enhance the design, colour and scenery of the film. Especially impressive is the show-piece ballroom scene, complete with 3-D crystal chandelier and 158 individual light sources to produce the effect of candles. With *T2* released in the same year, Hollywood finally sat up and took notice. 1991 also saw Lasseter make two short *Luxo, Jr* films for PBS' *Sesame Street*, including the sublime *Light and Heavy*.

In 1995, Pixar went public, beating Netscape as the biggest IPO of the year. It also saw *Toy Story* open on Thanksgiving weekend. This deceptively simple tale of the toys that are discarded after a birthday brings new friends was the highest grossing film of the year, pulling in over $500 million worldwide.

Pixar's story since then has seen them awarded prizes both for their technical achievements (Renderman, Digital Scanning, Digital Image Compositing) and, before the Oscar for best animated feature was created, half-arsed Oscar nominations for 'best original song' (*Toy Story 2*) and 'best musical or comedy score' (*A Bug's Life*).

What becomes apparent with each successive Pixar feature is that they can consistently reach the goals that they have set themselves. This doesn't just mean producing a film where the characters, story and action can engage an audience (although, given the many howlers in current animated features such as Disney's *Treasure Planet* (2002) and Dreamworks' *Sinbad* (2003), this is impressive enough). No, the devil really is in their detailing. For *A Bug's Life* (1998) it was light, for *Monsters Inc.* (2001), it was fur, and their latest, *Finding Nemo* (2003) it is was a realistic representation of water. Just looking at the motes drifting through the filtered light from 'above', all of it individually created, and you know that, just like the work of Tytla, Jones, Avery, Švankmajer, Quay, Godfrey, etc., you are in the presence of people who know their craft and want the world to share in the joy of their creation.

But *Toy Story* perhaps still remains their greatest achievement, for it had to prove that CGI animation could carry a feature-length film.

Other studios have not been slow to align themselves with CGI animation studios. DreamWorks have had impressive returns for their work with PDI: *Antz* (1998) and *Shrek* (2001). Fox, meanwhile, released Blue Sky's *Ice Age* (2001). While these films are enjoyable, and especially *Shrek*, they show that CGI is still evolving in convincingly representing reality – there are also warning signs of what is to come. *Jimmy Neutron Boy Genius* (2001) was a pilot film made by Nickelodeon. Produced using off-the-shelf CGI software packages like Messiah and Lightwave, it is visually unremarkable and narratively soulless. As CGI animation becomes cheaper and less time-consuming than traditional line or stop-motion animation it looks likely that many of the films will be as average as *Jimmy Neutron*. It's terrible to think that we've been spoilt so far. To use an analogy from early animation, let's hope that *Betty Boop* doesn't get supplanted by *Popeye* again.

The Death of Stop-Motion?

It was when stop-motion animation expert Phil Tippett saw test CGI footage for the dinosaur stampede in *Jurassic Park* he said that: 'It looked like the end'. Tippett, who had worked with the great Ray Harryhausen had developed 'go-motion' by which motion blur is added to stop-motion animated figures to clean out the jerkiness so infamous of the stop-motion technique. He wasn't completely on the scrapheap, however, for the CGI people needed his help in creating the Dinosaur Input Device (DID). What DID, ahem, did, was use an articulated dinosaur model with motion sensors attached to its limbs. Tippett moved the model in traditional stop-motion fashion and the motion was transmitted to the computer and recorded. This was then touched up by ILM and repeated as often as required using CGI techniques. All the same, one can't help feeling that Tippett could be the end of the line as far as Hollywood is concerned. In the UK, Oliver Postgate has retired but there remains Aardman and Nick Park (currently working on a feature-length Wallace and Gromit horror spoof) and the arcane Brothers Quay. Jan Švankmajer, although now mainly filming in live-action, still uses stop-motion sequences (*Little Otek* being the latest and most disturbing since *Alice*). The only remaining supporter in mainstream Hollywood is possibly director Joe Dante, who has used Tippett's skills for small sequences in most of his best films (*Piranha, The Howling, Gremlins*). I'll leave it for you to decide if his latest, *Looney Tunes – Back in Action* (2003), managed to breath life back into stop-motion or characters that have been mercilessly flogged to death over recent years in third-rate cash-ins and being milked as corporate logos for TimeWarner. (Daffy Duck – a *corporate logo*? Brrrr . . .)

The Simpsons and Beyond

'See, Marge, you knock TV and then it helps you out. I think you owe somebody a little apology.'

Homer Simpson

It began with a man who drew depressed rabbits for a living. Matt Groening (for it is he) was previously known as being part of a random collection of underground comic artists such as Lynda Barry, Mary Fleener and Gary Panter. With his syndicated comic strip *Life in Hell*, he detailed not only the lives of Binky (adult depressed rabbit), Sheba (adult female depressed rabbit) and Bongo (one-eared dysfunctional teen rabbit) but also the love/hate relationship of the little fezed men Akbar and Jeff. Oh, as well as taking swipes at pretty much every aspect of popular culture going. And all the characters had overbites, in case you wondered.

The world's most famous dysfunctional family started life as a series of short episodes on *The Tracey Ullman Show*. It first appeared on 19 April 1987 and ran in this format for three seasons until 14 May 1989. For the first two seasons, the stories were broken up over the length of the Ullman show but the third season saw the story being shown in one complete part. While the family looked extremely crude, many of the show's elements were introduced during these first three seasons, including secondary characters such as Krusty the Clown and Grampa Simpson. Also cemented here were Bart's catch-phrases ('Don't have a cow, man') that launched a thousand pirate t-shirts and the family tradition of Homer throttling Bart.

Originally animated by Klasky-Csupo, *The Simpsons* drew large viewing figures almost immediately. Its first full-length episode, *Simpsons Roasting by an Open Fire* (first broadcast 17 December 1989) also proved that an animated series could appeal to adults as well as children. What the series was particularly effective at was in realising a completely whole world where every citizen was a potential character, and not just the family Simpson. From Mr Burns, the evil, ancient nuclear-power plant owner to the Simpsons' good-natured Christian neigh-diddly-eighbour Ned Flanders, here was a town (the always-vaguely located Springfield) that bustled with life. Writers such as Conan O'Brien, John Swartzwelder and Jon Vitti helped create glorious scripts that were a smart mixture of social commentary and slapstick. Guest stars in the past have included Donald Sutherland, Danny DeVito, Sonic Youth and Rupert Murdoch among many, many others lining up to be given the trademark overbite. Coming soon, our own glorious leader, Tony Blair, will meet Homer Simpson, America's second dumbest citizen. Homer has mellowed a good deal since the early episodes when he was much more of a brute towards his family. But he has also become much more of a slapstick punchbag as well, which suggests that, while the series may not be running out of steam, its creativity could do with a good shake. *The*

Simpsons is now into its second decade and even a bad episode still carries enough ideas to hold your interest. Rupert Murdoch has credited it with having single-handedly saved Fox Television and it still fills many empty hours upon his Sky satellite station as well.

The Simpsons prevails, but Matt Groening's other pet-project *Futurama* (in which Fry, a cryogenically-frozen pizza-delivery boy from the twentieth century awakes in the thirtieth) was cancelled by Fox after its fifth season. This was a great shame, as its world was as well realised as that of *The Simpsons* and had the same mix of humour and filmic references. It also mixed standard cel animation with computer animation, producing some genuinely beautiful scenes – a rarity in television animation. It also had a thoroughly jaded view of the future in which the moon was a cheesy theme park and aliens could only be dissuaded from destroying earth by ensuring that they received new episodes of an Ally McBeal-like series.

Later on Fox came the incredibly smug (and very irritating) *Family Guy* (create by Seth McFarlane), which wanted to be *The Simpsons* meets Gary Larson's *The Far Side* (which was also briefly animated to reasonable effect) and crashed so loudly between these two stools it sounded like a bomb going off in a chair factory.

Simpsons original animators Klasky-Csupo also created several popular children's series, including *Rugrats*, *AAAHH! Real Monsters* and *The Wild Thornberrys*, all of which kept Nickelodeon in cartoons for some time. *Rugrats* and *The Wild Thornberrys* have both had successful spin-off movie careers, including a recent movie, *Rugrats Go Wild* (2003), where the two series collide. Klasky-

Csupo's most entertaining series was the liberal-baiting *Duckman*. Adapted from Everett Pack's comic book, the character was a lecherous, right-wing private eye, voiced by Jason Alexander (maintaining pretty much the same personality as he did for George Costanza in *Seinfeld*). Arguably the finest episode of this lovingly animated, deliberately twitchy series was the traditional clips episode, which seemed to rely entirely on playing back all of Duckman's finest rants and pseudo-swearing.

What was known as the 'new wave' of TV animation had already unofficially begun in 1987, with Ralph Bakshi's *The New Adventures of Mighty Mouse* which was directed with John Kricfalusi, whom we'll get to in a little while. *The New Adventures* famously ran into trouble when various small-minded right-wingers (including the Reverend Donald Wildmon) criticised a scene where Mighty Mouse was shown gaining strength by sniffing a flower as being a covert representation of sniffing cocaine. It has been rumoured that this scene closed the series but it ran for another season and a half before being cancelled. Bakshi already had a history of underground animation, including *Fritz the Cat* (1972) (which was disowned by the character's creator, Robert Crumb), *Heavy Traffic* (1973) and the worthy but problematically titled *Coonskin* (1974). Bakshi's later efforts included the first half of a projected two-part adaptation of *The Lord of the Rings* (1978) which relied heavily upon rotoscoping for many of its characters. The first part was so badly received that the second half never gained the necessary finance. He also made the extremely poor *Cool World* (1992), an attempt to make an adult-themed *Who Framed Roger Rabbit?* – featuring Brad

Pitt and Gabriel Byrne. While it contained some enjoyable moments, the overall effect was of low-grade humour and mismatched live-action/animation sequences.

Fired by this renewed interest in TV animation, many animators rebelled against the predictability of series produced by Filmation and Hanna-Barbera, what John Kricfalusi termed as 'non-cartoon cartoons' (in that the characters may as well be played by live actors for all the unexplored potential of cartoonishness these series displayed). Instead, many of them returned to their own influences, the likes of Tex Avery and the 'limited animation' style of UPA. However, that didn't stop cynical corporate monstrosities like *Tiny Toons* and *Animaniacs* being made.

The king of all new animation is John Kricfalusi's *The Ren and Stimpy Show*, which coupled cel slapstick with gruesomely detailed limited animation frames. A traditional cat and dog act that was anything but traditional, Ren was a volcanic-tempered Chihuahua and Stimpy was a large stupid cat. They shared a bed and lived in a world populated with Muddy the Mudskipper TV shows (a mickey-take of formulaic Hanna-Barbera cartoons), overtly sexualised women (*a la* Tex Avery) and other oddities. Combining gross-out humour with twisted characterisation, its finest moments were *Son of Stimpy* in which Stimpy farts and, believing he has given birth, spends the rest of the episode searching for his long-lost child (who turns up at the end, to ask Stimpy's permission to marry a rotting fish head) and *Ren's Toothache*. I defy anyone to come up with anything, animated or otherwise, that is more horrifying and nightmarishly funny than this episode (and I include *Eraserhead*). Schools should show it instead of handing out dental hygiene leaflets. It has the queasy quality of Freudian dreams about ageing, but you don't wake up at the end – it just hangs there at the back of your mind, stinky gums and all. Needless to say, Kricfalusi didn't last long at Nickelodeon. After running into various censorship problems over the show (including a thick-witted complaint about the name of the character George Liquor) and drastic editing of his original storyboards, Kricfalusi left. Nickelodeon retained the copyright to *Ren and Stimpy* and swiftly turned it into just what Kricfalusi had been rebelling against: a Hanna-Barbera cartoon where the main characters did a lot of running around and were just punchbags for various episodes of dull-humoured slapstick; the sort of thing that only a corporation could love. Kricfalusi would later launch his animated series *Weekend Pussy Hunt* and *The Goddamn George Liquor Program* on the Internet. His return to television was *The Ripping Friends* (a superhero spoof) for Fox Kids in 2001.

Nickelodeon later launched the *Ren and Stimpy*-lite cartoon series *Rocko's Modern Life* and the quirkier *SpongeBob SquarePants*.

MTV's *Liquid Television* (first aired in 1991) was a 'various artists' package of animated work and usually had something worth seeing (particularly Richard Sala's *Invisible Hands* which successfully brought his macabre comic strips to life) but soon became bogged down in too many third-rate serials instead of quirky one-offs. The station had more success with *Celebrity Death-Match* which pitted claymation celebrities against each other. Probably their finest hour came with *Beavis and Butthead* wherein two dim teens sat watching the tube and snickering uncontrollably at music videos, spliced in with actual storylines where they'd try to do something and make a complete mess of it. It had a spin-off, of sorts, in *Daria*, about the smartest girl at their school. More entertaining was the feature film, *Beavis and Butthead Do America* in which their TV gets stolen and they embark on a road trip across the States to try to find it. *Beavis* animator Mike Judge had originally come to attention on *Liquid Television* and his later series, again using the UPA style of limited animation, was *King of the Hill*, focusing on a marginal *Beavis* character, Hank Hill. A salesman of 'propane and propane accessories' in Texas, Hill was an inspired tragicomic creation. Surrounded by his dim (and often unintelligible) friends, and his dysfunctional family, Hill's life was painfully and lovingly realised by Judge. Each episode was shot-through with the character's pride in his achievements while still being vaguely aware of the emptiness of it all. It deserved much better treatment than the schedules gave it and remains probably the most adult of this new wave of animation.

At the other end of the scale came Comedy Central's *South Park* by Trey Parker and Matt Stone. Parker and Stone had been contracted to make the series after an animated Christmas card they made featuring Santa Claus and Jesus battling for supremacy over the meaning of Christmas had done the Hollywood rounds. *South Park* focuses on four children: Jewish Kyle, jittery Stan, muffled-by-anorak Kenny (who always dies in each episode but is resurrected for the next) and complete bastard Eric

Cartman. Around them revolve a small Colorado community of completely screwed-up adults. Its first broadcast episode was *Cartman Gets an Anal Probe* – which pretty much set out its stall as far as humour goes. But, beneath the fart gags and the gross-outs, there lurks a razor-sharp wit, laced with a certain amount of liberalism. Like Bart Simpson, only more so, these are little kids behaving often how little kids behave – especially the bullying Cartman, who bestows and snatches away his friendship like it is a yoyo. When Kenny was finally killed properly in *Kenny Dies*, it was surprisingly moving, even though the animators claimed that they had just got bored with inventing ways to kill him off. Particularly special is the movie *South Park – Bigger, Longer and Uncut* with proper (and, I'm ashamed to admit, very funny) swearing, Saddam Hussein and Satan setting up house together, the US declaring war against Canada and several wonderful songs parodying the Disney tradition (including *Blame Canada* which nearly won an Oscar, and a worthwhile reprise of Cartman's popular ditty *Kyle's Mom is a Bitch*).

Cartoon Network, the cable station devoted to rerunning Warner and Hanna-Barbera cartoons, began producing its own series in 1993 with *2 Stupid Dogs* (created by Donovan Cook, who had briefly worked on *Ren and Stimpy*). Later series included David Feiss' immortal *Cow and Chicken* and Van Partible's less impressive *Johnny Bravo*. There were also Danny Antonucchi's variable *Ed, Edd N Eddy*, John Dilworth's intermittently weird *Courage the Cowardly Dog* and Mo Willems' tiresome *Sheep in the Big City*. Probably the most enjoyable and risk-taking work produced by Cartoon Network came from Craig McCracken and Genndy Tartakovsky. Both had attended an experimental animation programme at CalArts and their bold, colourful style yielded *The Powerpuff Girls* (McCracken's apparent repositioning of anime for an American audience, with vivid colours, stylised violence and super-powered schoolgirls) and *Dexter's Laboratory* (Tartakovsky's equally colourful gag-machine featuring a boy-genius and his inadvertently destructive sister, DeeDee). Tartakovsky has since progressed to the visually stunning *Samurai Jack*, where, having been trapped in the future by a demon, a samurai travels the world, battling evil. The action sequences, frequently morphing into widescreen format, are beautifully choreographed and graphically violent — acceptable to TV only on the grounds that the victims are usually androids and spurt oil rather than blood.

The British equivalents have been extremely variable: the tedious *Stressed Eric*, and *Rex the Runt* which was slightly better (and from Aardman, who also produced the claymation Internet-only *Angry Kid*). *Bob and Margaret* was a so-so spin-off of *Bob's Birthday* (co-financed by Comedy Central) and *Pond Life* dealt with a neurotic single woman's relationships before Bridget Jones cornered the market. All of these have since been cancelled. Currently, as well as the satirical *2-D-TV*, there is the patchy 'surreal sketch show' *Monkey Dust*. Some of the styles on show are worth seeing, but the best gags aren't always connected with the best animation. And they've still to come up with anything as spiteful as Renwick and Marshall's attack on Hanna-Barbera, 'Cheapo Cartoon-man' in the live-action sketch show *End of Part One*.

Outside of children's TV, small screen animation appears to have slowed down. The cancellation of *Futurama* suggested that no one was immune. While Nick Park and Aardman have recently made interlude-length episodes of *Wallace and Gromit* and *Creature Comforts* for BBC and Channel 4 respectively, but both channels, investment in animation as a whole appears to have been cut back dramatically since the early 90s when the likes of Švankmajer and the Quay Brothers were being commissioned to produce works for TV.

Animator's Dozen

As if the previous films mentioned weren't enough to whet your appetite, here's a further baker's dozen that I didn't find room to mention properly for one reason or another and come thoroughly recommended:

Animal Farm (1955, Dirs: John Halas, Joy Batchelor) Despite eschewing Orwell's anti-Stalinist novel's bleak ending for something more upbeat, Halas & Batchelor's adaptation remains a landmark of British feature animation. When the tyrannical farmer is overthrown by the animals, the pigs begin to insinuate their own equally tyrannical regime. Likewise, Halas & Batchelor overthrew the producer's intended propaganda movie in favour of a dark and atmospheric meditation on the nature of freedom. Animal Farm also showed that one could learn Disney's lessons and still retain one's own artistic identity.

Fantastic Planet (*La Planète Sauvage*, 1973. Dir: René Lalou) While Lalou's plot (co-written with Roland Topor) is basically a rewrite of David versus Goliath, the animation and the design of this film are coherently realised. The tiny Oms are kept as pets by the gigantic Draags until one of the little folk unites the others in a savage rebellion.

The Secret Adventures of Tom Thumb (1993, Dir: David

Borthwick) Combining elements of the fairy-tale with more modern ecological and humanist concerns, Borthwick's stop-motion feature is both moving and chilling in turns.

The Diabolical Invention (*Vynalez Zkazy*, 1958, Dir: Karel Zeman) A breathtaking mixture of live-action, animation, puppetry and glass painting that is a poetic evocation of Jules Verne's writings. Zeman brings to the screen 3-D recreations of etched illustrations from an early edition of Verne's works, including a remarkable submarine. Zeman later directed a superior adaptation of the Baron Munchausen stories, entitled *Baron Prasil* (1961).

Special Delivery (1978, Dir: John Weldon) Allegedly created to demonstrate to Canadian postal workers the benefits of joining the Letter Carriers Union, this cheerfully morbid little tale involves a dead, naked postman, evasion of justice, an adulterous wife and a man who wouldn't sweep the snow from his driveway.

The Big Snit (1985, Dir: Richard Condie) Or, how to show the devastation of a nuclear holocaust by comparing it to a domestic argument over cheating at Scrabble. Truly demented fare from NFBC. 'Don't you shake your eyes at me!'

Evolution (1971, Dir: Michael Mills) Another NFBC classic, detailing the evolution of life on a strange planet. Charles Darwin with jokes, the message appears to be along the lines of 'survival of the weirdest'.

The Sandman (1991, Dir: Paul Berry) And you thought all Cosgrove-Hall output was anthropomorphism with bad puns (*Danger Mouse, Count Duckula*). A short, sharp adaptation of the E T A Hoffman story with a gruesome climax, it also includes flawless stop-motion work, especially in the sequence where a small child climbs a rickety staircase.

Waking Life (2001, Dir: Richard Linklater and Bob Sabiston) Spooky-woozy dreamscape philosophizing from Linklater and animator Sabiston – a kind of *Little Nemo* meets *Slacker* and proof that there's still life in old techniques. All the actors were filmed and then rotoscoped producing an innovative and deliberately digressive film. It doesn't work all the time but it's always beautiful to look at.

Push Comes to Shove (1992, Dir: Bill Plympton) Had I room enough and time, Bill Plympton would have had a proper entry, but this is his finest moment: two men meet and inflict horrifying cartoon violence on each other until someone goes too far. Other Plympton cartoons worth tracking down include: *25 Ways to Quit Smoking* and *One of Those Days*.

The Black Dog (1987, Dir: Alison De Vere) Lyrical and autobiographical animation about a journey through mythological aspects of womanhood to self-discovery. The mystical elements are deftly handled, ensuring the film never becomes willfully obscure.

Deadsy/ Door (1990, Dir: David Anderson) Animated adaptations of Russell Hoban's macabre wordplay that uses stop-motion and animated photographs to produce two genuinely otherworldly shorts.

The Hill Farm (1989, Dir: Mark Baker) is Baker's thoughtful look at life at the sharp end of agriculture. Its sympathetic handling of its characters' lives is never at the expense of missing out on a few sharp jokes at the expense of the hunt, townies, etc.

Resources

Books

Le Masters Of Animation, John Grant, UK, B T Batsford, 2001
Glossy title with many rare stills, giving leisurely biographies of many key animators, including McCay, Disney, the Fleischers and Paul Terry.

Understanding Animation by Paul Wells, UK, Routledge, 1998
Accessible film studies guide to aspects of animation, including issues of representation and narrative structure.

7 Minutes: The Life and Death of the American Cartoon, Norman M Klein, UK, Verso, 1993
Klein's scholarly work runs from the early days up to UPA and Hanna-Barbera, giving a breakdown of themes, obsessions and historical context to the 'golden age' of cartoons.

Cartoons: One Hundred Years Of Cinema Animation, Giannalberto Bendazzi, UK, John Libbey & Company, 1994

Exhaustive global survey of animation, covering up to 1993. Bendazzi is enthusiastic and concise which is all too the good, given the scope of the book. The only drawback is that the index insists on listing films that begin with 'The' under 'T'. Hope you've got a good memory for the definite article . . .

The Anime Encyclopedia: A Guide to Japanese Animation since 1917, Jonathan Clements and Helen McCarthy, US, Stone Bridge Press, 2001
The title says it all, the most up to date guide on anime currently available.

The Animation Book: A Complete Guide To Animated Filmmaking – From Flip Books to Sound Cartoons to 3-D Animation, Kit Laybourne, US, Three Rivers Press, 1998
Another self-descriptive book, this one is ideal if you're keen to make your own animation and need to start from scratch.

Prime Time Animation, Carole A Stabile and Mark Hanson, UK, Routledge, 2003
Almost a companion to Wells' book, this title considers TV animation from Hanna-Barbera to *The Simpsons* up to the present.

Internet Sites

Many animation studios have their own dedicated sites. Some of the best include Pixar's (www.pixar.com), with downloadable Quicktime versions of their short films (although the studio's biography can be a little overwhelming); Aardman (www.aardman.com) also has downloadable shorts, as well as 'making of' spots, while Warner Brothers (www.wbanimation.com) is loud, colourful and has several rather loopy games.

For more varied coverage and all the latest news and gossip, you could do worse than to check out the following sites, which between them pretty much cover most aspects of animation: Cartoon Network (www.cartoonnetwork.com), Animation World Network (www.awn.com) and The Big Cartoon Database (www.bcdb.com).

That's all folks!